You, DAD!

The world needs real DADS.

The Most Powerful Man In The World

Copyright © 2013 Chris Royce

ISBN- 978-0-9886854-0-6

All rights reserved. Printed in the United States of America. Reproduction of contents and /or cover in whole or in part in any form is strictly prohibited without the expresse written consent of the publisher.

Published by
Dominion Kingdom Publishers
West Henrietta, New York
johdmgsui@me.com

Edited by Dianne Ogden

For additional copies of this book, please send correspondence to:

Web: www.themostpowerfulman.com

Contents

Acknowledgments		7
Forewords		9
Introduction		15
Chapter 1:	Answer Their Questions	23
Chapter 2:	The Patience Perspective	29
Chapter 3:	Serious DAD Silly DAD	37
Chapter 4:	Never, Always, & The One Thing We Must Keep	51
Chapter 5:	Fight for Their Hearts	61
Chapter 6:	The 8 x 18 Factor	93
Chapter 7:	All Kids Are Broke	115
Chapter 8:	Faith & Forgiveness	133
The Top Five Things To Pray About For Your Kids		139
A Few Family Favorites		142
A Random List of Really Crappy Things		143
Resources		145

This book is dedicated to Olivia and Nate.
The joy you bring me every day
is not able to be put in words.
I love you!

Acknowledgements

I would like to thank my wife, Sherri, for your support and encouragement in writing this book, and for always holding down the fort for so many years. I have been free to do what I needed to do, and without you, it wouldn't have been possible.

I would also like to thank my Band of Brothers who are the coolest, toughest, and strangest group of men you'll ever meet. Your encouragement and brotherhood means the world to me. You are all so dedicated to helping men be real men, husbands and DADS.

The Band Of Brothers: Ricky Allman, Jose Batalla, Jim Beaulne, Dan Breckenridge, Johnny Burchfield, Dewey Cass, Nathan Downs, Eric Dubbell, Mark Edwards, Asaad Faraj, Dave Farmer, Frank Giglio, Dallas Gooden, Aaron Halterman, Kenny Hughes, Jeff Johnson, Chris Koob, Steve Minter, Herb Padilla, Mark Penny, Alex Ruzich, Mike Sharpe, Guy Shashaty, Sam Shepard, John Smith, Turbo, Tom Varano (My oldest and original friend in this world!), George Verdugo, Ron Wolter, and Mark Younger.

I want to thank Mike Tuttle, for giving me Wild at Heart back in 2003. The chain reaction that was created by that gift is absolutely amazing. Also, thank you to John Eldredge, for your courage and insight. So many lives and families have been changed as a result of what you do.

Thank you to Jeff LeFevre. We made a major impact in each other's lives when we were much younger. What you gave me has helped me to this day, and in being a world class DAD.

There are a few other men that have made a real difference in my life. I appreciate Rick Doyle, Bill Orender, Bill Whittle, and Jim Kocher for what they have done for me personally and in my business life over the years.

Thank you to Dianne Ogden for your expertise and enthusiasm. I appreciate your effort so much!

I would like to thank Jamie House for your input and guidance on this project. You are a true brother and a great friend.

And lastly, thank you DAD, for the time you spent with me as a boy. I remember the time in the woods, scouts, and all the backyard sports.

Foreword

Webster's Dictionary defines father as, "a male parent." While this is an accurate definition, Webster's Dictionary fails to acknowledge the rest of what fathers are, especially to their little kids.

They're the ones that give us piggy back rides up the stairs when we're too tired to walk ourselves, the ones that read us bedtime stories, or laugh at our jokes that make no sense, or sit through our third grade music concert because we're so pumped about our xylophone solo, or teach us how to put gas in the car. We are simply wired as kids to see our DADS as our leaders, our role models, and our best buddies.

I've intimately known my DAD my whole life. He's always been right there next to me through my best and worst moments. When that kid threw up on my bus and I thought I was scarred for life, he talked me through the emotional suffering. When I fell head first into a pile of gravel, he explained to the nurse what happened so I didn't have to bear the embarrassment.

When I got the stomach flu two days before my black belt ceremony, he prayed with me. When he offered me fifty bucks to sing Christmas carols to the diners at Olive Garden as a joke, and I did it, he paid me anyway. He never let me down no matter how ridiculous I may have acted. It's because he's faithful.

I've never once doubted the unconditional love my DAD has for me. I remember when I was little I wanted to marry him! I envied my mom. In my eyes she had the one symbol of true love – marriage. At the time he was the only boy I didn't think was gross. As he showed me the love and attention that a little girl needs from her daddy, I developed an unconditional love for him. It's because he is affectionate.

My DAD is the one person that understands me best. We think the same way. He can talk me through pretty much anything and I know I can come to him with anything. I can say that I've always envisioned our relationship as unbreakable, and I know that it is that way today because he is caring.

He's also the only one that can truly make me belly laugh. Every time we're together, we find a way to laugh about something. Our sense of humor brings us closer together. I can't imagine a serious, all business DAD! I look forward to the moments when we laugh and our stomach hurts when we're finally done. I cherish those moments because he makes me thankful for the fact that I'm able to laugh and have fun with my family. It's all because he's silly.

I know that within all of the DADS out there there's a faithful, affectionate, caring, silly guy that wants to break free for his kids. I can say from personal experience that your kids want a relationship with you. And if there's anyone that you should listen to about becoming an even better DAD that you naturally are, it's mine! I thank God every day for the daddy he is and the daddy He gave me.

-Olivia Royce, Age 14

The Most Powerful Man In The World

I'm writing this forword for not only my dad, but all of the dads that are just starting out, or want to improve, or just be great dads!

I love my dad so much. I love the fact that he is always there for me, just like you should be for your son or daughter. I also like the fact that he always pertects me, like when I'm sledding and he stands in the way so I don't smash into the trees, and in the summer when I face plant into the grass he is the first one to help me up. The most important thing is that he spends time with me and plays with me, like building robots and drawing pictures and even sitting down and whatching wipeout or a cool animal show. all that fun dosen't take much time. Enjoy the Book!!!

Nate Royce
- age 10

Chris Royce

Ode to DADS

The lion of the den
The eagle of the air
The great white of the sea
The "P" in protection

Holding me tight from day one
Watching me close with eyes like a hawk
Giving me faith
Showing me my place

Walking ahead
But staying near
Watching his cubs
Like a great black bear

A father is there
To guide my path
And show me the way

His kind words
Make me feel special
Deep inside

The leader of the pack
The confidence bearer
The rock of my world

-Olivia Royce
Age 10

THE PROMISE

You can be a world class DAD. You can maximize the immense joys and hit the tough challenges head on. You can give your children what they need and you can be their hero. This book will tell you how to live the dream as a DAD, and your family will never be the same.

The Dream

We have to ask ourselves, what is the dream when it comes to DAD-hood? We know what the dream is in sports... It's cutting the net at the Big Dance, the Super Bowl Ring, the Stanley Cup, and the World Series. It's the winners circle at the Daytona 500, the podium for Olympic Gold, the Green Jacket at the Masters!

We know the dream in academics... it's the scholarship, the published works, Ph.D. In business it's the start-up that goes public, the penny stock that hits big, or the family business that grows from generation to generation. Hollywood and entertainers covet the Oscar, the Emmy, the Grammy and Tony.

What about family and us, DADS? What is the dream and is there any guarantee that it's going to be worth it? How do we know we are on the right track in this life long endeavor of being a world class DAD?

I think the Holy Grail of fathering is revealed in a few things:

- It's when your 5 year old puts on your shoes, mimics your stance, and then walks around the house behind you.

- It's when you get notes, pictures and cards left on your pillow.

- It's when you're driving in the car and your 10 year old son starts crying right out of the blue. Then he tells you it's because he loves you so much, and he's thankful to have the best DAD in the world.

- It's when the neighborhood kids congregate in your garage and don't want to leave.

- It's when other adults tell you they are so impressed with your kids and the way they shake their hand and look them right in the eye.

- It's when your kids make good choices and you know it.

- It's when your kids make bad choices and they tell you.

- It's when they talk about being married and having kids of their own, but they are still in elementary school.

- It's when your teenage daughter has enough confidence and self respect to say "no".

- It's when your kids show respect to their mother because you do.

- It's when you make them laugh so hard they cry.

- It's when they make you laugh so hard you cry.

- It's when they fight through their challenges because you did.

- It's when they choose a great career path and spouse, and have a family of their own.

- It's when they look you in the eye as an adult and say, "Thank you."

Introduction

It was pitch black. The kind of thick, heavy darkness that clings to you and everything around you. The kind where you can't see your hand six inches in front of your face. The heat and humidity added to the intensity. Around me a collection of sounds rose up in a chorus of musicians from all walks of the kingdom.

There were strange birds that shrieked much more than sang, invisible insects whose bodies couldn't have possibly matched their huge sounds, and the dominant section of this eerie orchestra... howler monkeys. Their collective sounds filled the night like the largest of factories clamoring and grinding at the edge of a city.

It was after 11 p.m. We had already been up for 18 hours, spending most of that time Peacock bass fishing in 115 degrees. Now we were hunting caimans. No one was sleepy. We were somewhere in Central Brazil. The Amazon River is a remarkably vast waterway; it carries more water than any other river on the planet. It's over 1200 miles longer than the Mississippi.

There were three of us Americans and two local guides on the small bass boat. Our guides spoke Portuguese, and we didn't. But we all knew the mission, and the plan was fairly simple. Jorge, our lead guide, had the ultimate high tech search light... a car headlight strapped to his straw hat, and attached to a car battery on the floor of the boat. Very resourceful. He would slowly scan the shoreline and we'd pick out pairs of orange glowing eyes reflecting in the light.

Once they were spotted, Jorge would then head towards them – cut the motor – and we'd silently drift in.

Quietly, carefully, two of us would get ready with the noose. All we had was a 5' hollow metal pole with a steel cable running through it, with a noose on the end. One guy stood on the bow and slowly lowered the ring around the snout of the caiman. The guy behind him would pull the cable for all he was worth, cinching the noose around the caiman's nose. Hopefully. If the gator lunged forward and the cable cinched around its belly instead, we had an issue.

These specimens ranged from 3' to 7' in length. They were certainly large enough to take off fingers and hands, so we had to pay attention. After catching a couple, and releasing them, it was my turn at the helm. We glided into a spot with our sights on a smaller one, about 3 feet or so. As we moved in, there were branches in the way that made it impossible for me to lower the noose.

Jorge was saying, "Hand, hand." In the heat of the adrenalin filled moment, and my assuming I knew what he was saying, I dropped the pole and went over the front of the boat like a wild man. I grabbed that caiman right behind the back of the head and plucked him up out of the water with a huge splash, and a mouth full of mud. I opened my eyes (Yes, I admit it.) and turned around to see the two locals and my two buddies with their mouths wide open.

The only thing I could think of to say was… "That's the way we do it in New York!"

Come to find out, our Brazilian friend was trying to say, "I'll give you a hand moving the branches." Not, "Hey white guy from New York, reach into the Amazon River in the middle of the night and catch a wild caiman with your bare hands."

I guess things can get lost in translation. Or maybe it's just because men are like that. We're wired to be out there doing something, prone to not listening, and eager to impress. My Amazon adventure was one of the best trips of my life. It was exciting, challenging, fun, and intense.

Just like being a DAD. Or like being a DAD should be. I've wanted to write this book for a long time. The thoughts and ideas contained in it are simple; however, I have learned that many of life's simple concepts and ideas are actually quite profound.

> **"True genius resides in simplicity."**
> **-Albert Einstein**

I have traveled around the country and spoken to thousands of people, particularly DADS. I have been consistently amazed by the response to these simple ideas, and how they can affect a relationship between a father and his son or daughter.

It is also amazing to me that so many men have dropped the ball as DADS. There is nothing worse than a dead beat DAD. The American family has been under assault for decades now, and too many DADS have been taken out. Our little girls need daddies. Our sons need fathers.

A father's influence cannot be replaced. It is critical to the strength and future of your family, your community, and our country. I hope you are ready to step up DAD… You are desperately needed!

Chris Royce

You've Been Blessed!

What an incredible gift it is to have children. There are so many couples around the world that would give anything to have a child... or to have their child back. Hopeful parents go through great lengths to start families through adoption and in vitro procedures. There are over 125,000 adoptions in the US every year, and over 5,000,000 Americans are adoptees. The foster care system exceeds 500,000 children under the age of 18.

Every year almost 250,000* babies are born worldwide through in vitro. On average, the cost of in vitro fertilization is approximately $12,000.00 per cycle, and the success rate for women under the age of thirty-six is only 35.7%**. Fathers who become fathers through in vitro start with an advantage. They want it. Want it badly enough to work for it.

In vitro is planned, calculated, expensive, and stressful. It is a huge commitment that can sometimes make or break a marriage. For couples that embark on the journey and see it through to the prize – a live birth – their reward is almost beyond measure. The special journey these parents travel results in real appreciation for being a parent. This is something they don't take for granted.

For parents who may have tried in vitro and it didn't work, or realized early on they answered to a higher calling, there is adoption. There are parents who make the conscious effort to open their hearts, maybe a little wider than the rest of us, and welcome the responsibility of caring for another human being not of their own flesh and blood.

*Source: European Society for Human Reproduction & Embryology, May 2009
**Source: Official SART statistics 2010

The Most Powerful Man In The World

What greater gift could a parent give, than to open their heart to a child and accept them as their own? So, quite simply, what lies at the heart of being a great DAD is something simple and profound - be thankful for your children.

I have a deep sense of awe and wonder that I had something to do with the creation of another human being... a beautiful, unique, one-of-a-kind person with a purpose on earth. Wow! I am also aware that I am responsible for the care, provision and development of this precious gift of life.

When you start from a position of genuine gratitude for your children, you will find patience you never knew you had and the coping mechanisms to deal with the challenges and trying times in a much better way. Our perspective is so important. It's easier to be patient, kind, and understanding when we are thankful.

Let's face it DADS, we've all blown a gasket and then wondered why. We ask ourselves, "Why did that make me so mad? Why can't I be more patient? Why do I sound so much like my DAD?" It's usually because our perspective gets a bit twisted.

We will discuss the Patience Perspective in a later chapter, and how to adjust our thinking to become more patient, but the first cornerstone is, have a thankful heart.

If you are a DAD, you've been blessed, and it's up to you to become the best DAD in the world. Your kids need that from you. This book was created to help you achieve that goal, and you can do it.

I hope you find the thoughts, ideas and stories in these pages helpful, challenging, humorous, and moving. I have capitalized the word DAD throughout the entire book to remind you how important you are. In between chapters I have included original notes and cards that I have received from my two children over the years. They have not been spell-checked and may contain grammatical errors. The artwork is... well, interesting to say the least. But they are genuine, original and heartfelt. They represent the fruit of the massive effort. They prove it's worth it, and that to our children, we are the most powerful man in the world.

Enjoy!

"That's the way we do it in New York!"

"Jorge and his high tech searchlight on the hunt."

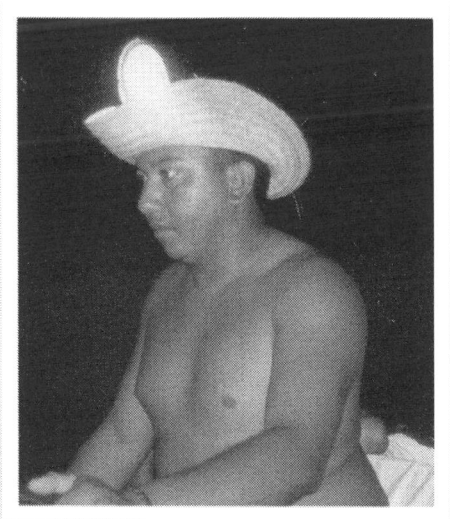

Chris Royce

Chapter One

Answer Their Questions

In 2003 I read a book that absolutely changed my life. It is called "Wild at Heart", by John Eldredge. (I suggest you pick it up and read it!) One of the most profound realizations I had as I read that book deals with the fundamental questions we have wired into our hearts from birth.

We all have them, and it's up to fathers to answer them. For boys, "Am I the apple of your eye?" and "Do I have what it takes?" For girls, "Am I lovely?" and "Do you see me?"

Wow! How obvious this should be, but sadly it isn't. Did your DAD answer those questions for you as a young boy? Did you know that you were the apple of his eye? Did he affirm and reaffirm over and over again that "you have what it takes"? Probably not. Unfortunately, probably not. It's because no one did that for him. It's God's design that masculinity is bestowed from a father to a son. It's God's design that a father answers his son's fundamental questions about his manhood. It's also God's design that a father affirms his daughter's femininity and makes sure she knows she is lovely, - that he sees her.

The evidence is clear. The longing for answers to these questions comes out at a very early age. Little boys desperately want their daddy to be proud of them, tell them they are strong, fast, clever, and tough.

How damaging is it when this doesn't happen? It's even more tragic when the opposite happens. Haven't you seen the over- compensation in the weight room, or on the field? You must have met a bully or two in your day. You know the driven, arrogant, "I don't need anybody" guy.

> "Behind every posing man, there is a wounded boy."
> -John Eldredge, Wild at Heart

Typically, these guys started as little boys who never got their questions answered. Now they are trapped in men's bodies- still searching. "Behind every posing man, there is a wounded boy." -John Eldredge, Wild at Heart

You've also seen young girls, dating the wrong guys, latching on to the first male who shows them attention. What they hear is; "You are lovely, and I see you." The boyfriend probably doesn't see anything but her body. But to her, his attention answers a fundamental question- "Do you see me?" At least that's her perception. Her boyfriend is giving her the answer she never got from her father.

The Most Powerful Man In The World

The woman on the pole at the strip club… just a little girl who is still wondering deep inside "Am I lovely, do you see me?" Or maybe it's become "**Now** you see me!"

The submerged anger, bitterness and pain have driven her to that performance. She may not even realize that's what it is.

No wonder the divorce rate is so high. I believe it's largely because these tragic, broken hearts and relationships continue for generations. However, I also believe they can be mended. The curse of the unanswered questions can end with you and your beautiful children. Starting today you can answer your son's questions. Starting today you can build your daughter's self esteem and emotional stability by answering her questions. It doesn't matter how old they are, they still want to hear it. They still *need* to hear it.

What nicknames do you have for your son? Do you greet him with a huge smile, and a "Good morning, Wild Man!" or tuck him in with a "Sleep tight, Handsome?" How about, "See you in the morning, stud! I'm proud of you. You're a great son." There's no limit to the number of times we should answer his questions.

How often do you tell your daughter she's a real beauty? She's graceful, smart, fun. Your praise will set the standard for any boys she will spend time with. Set it high, you will protect her. Set it low, you will expose her.

There will come a time when your son will be tested. He will have to prove he has what it takes. When this happens, he will need to draw from the well of encouragement you've filled for him. We can intentionally create opportunities for our sons to prove themselves capable so, when we aren't there, they will have some wins under their belt.

Create a challenge that is age appropriate and realistic. Don't be too quick to help him through it, but be there for him. His confidence will soar.

A few ideas:
- A challenging hike in the woods
- A back yard obstacle course
- If you are handy, an appropriate building project
- Build a camp fire (And get it going without gasoline!)
- Fishing works great (Just make sure there are fish in the lake!)

It doesn't have to be physical, but I don't think video games are a way to show boys they have what it takes to be a man. Take some time to find something that is a good fit for you and your son.

I want to discuss dealing with other people's kids. We have a great opportunity in our everyday lives to affirm and encourage other children besides our own. Why not be the neighborhood hero? I'm sure there are kids around with unanswered questions. Even if the DADS on your block are great DADS, why not share your qualities and knowledge with their kids. It will reinforce what these kids are already getting at home.

Whenever I talk to a child, especially a younger one say 2 – 5 years old, I always try to get down, eye to eye, to their level. I do this any time a young child comes to my office with their parents. I always take a knee. It's a subtle way to build them up. Think about it... kids get tired of looking up at adults all the time. When I get down on one knee and look them in the eye, they feel bigger. And all kids want to feel bigger! When a kid from the neighborhood is walking up the driveway, I greet them the same way I would greet my own kids in the morning or after school. Maybe that day their DAD wasn't around when they left the house. Maybe they had a tough day at school, or their DAD was working late. A simple up- beat greeting of "Hey wild man – how's it going?!" will make them feel a bit better.

When little girls in the neighborhood ride up on their bikes I say, "Wow that's a pretty dress!" The reaction is always the same. It's a huge smile. I try to be out at the curb in the morning before the school bus leaves. As my kids and their neighborhood friends line up, I like to compliment them and encourage them before they leave. It's one way for me to give back to the people around me, and make a small impact in a positive way, even when these kids have great parents.

It makes a much bigger impact in the lives of kids who have parents who aren't so great. The kid in your neighborhood with the dead-beat DAD and the broken home needs you to answer his/her questions. And you can, if you're willing.

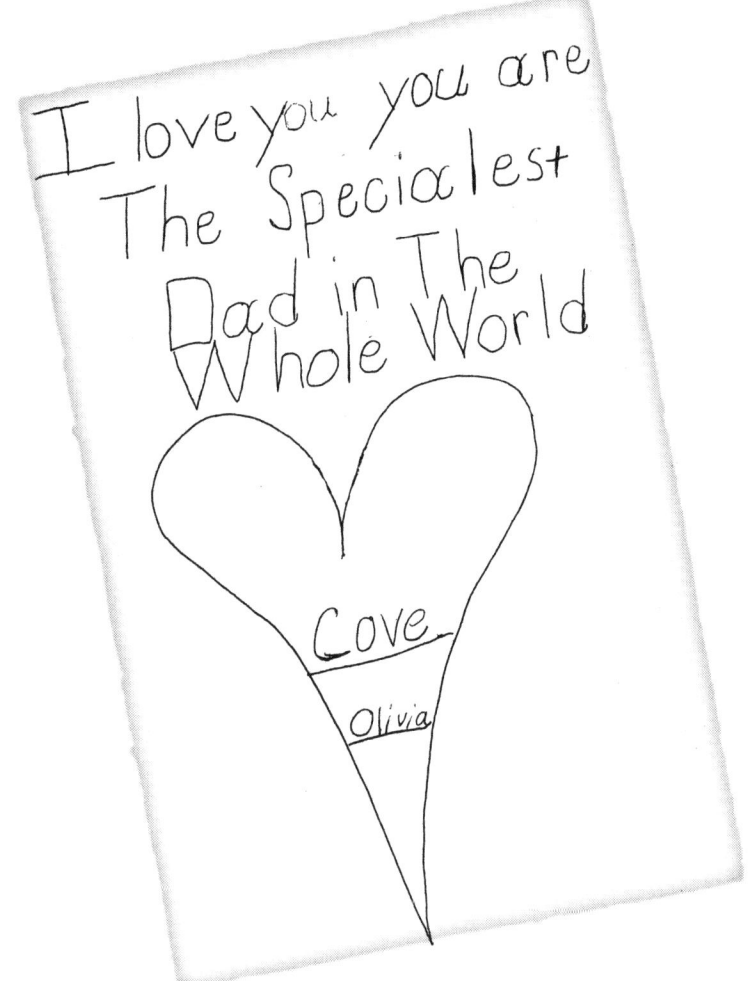

Chapter Two

The Patience Perspective

How many of us grew up with impatient DADS? It seemed like our DADS were always aggravated. We never knew when our DAD would lose his temper, or why. This can have a *great* effect on young children and their confidence. I believe we should never grow up afraid of our DADS. We should respect our DADS and understand that they have tremendous power, but we should never be afraid. Our kids should never ever be afraid of us.

I think our sons need to see strength and kindness in the same package. Our daughters need to see fierceness and tenderness together. The strength and the fierceness we show is not directed towards our children, but rather it is protective, directed towards forces outside our family that would attempt to disrupt our relationships.

I believe we should show our children kindness and tenderness with the hope that they will come to understand our strength and fierceness is directed outwardly, towards anything that threatens the family. Kindness and tenderness draws them so much closer to us. I see little evidence that being harsh, overly strict, overbearing or impatient with children is fruitful.

So many DADS and parents are reactionary. When you were a little boy with your DAD and all you wanted was for him to be with you, how often did that precious time get stolen because he was so impatient? There were probably too many times as a little boy you tried to help him out while he was fixing the car, or working on some household project, when the joy in that experience evaporated because, ultimately, he snapped over something insignificant.

You may have been afraid if you spilled something or dropped something you'd catch the wrath of your DAD. Most of the time the project itself was far less important than the time you spent together. It may have been a great chance to learn a valuable lesson that would serve you later in life.

How many times do we feel tired, and our patience is worn thin? We end up sending a message to our precious little kids – you're bothering us. We snap at them if they interrupt us while we are working on something. Maybe they were just trying to just show us a little picture they drew or they wanted to tell us something, and what's our reply? We are harsh towards them. Then we feel terrible afterwards...

So, how can we make a shift and become more patient as DADS? I think we have to zero in on this concept of patience. What an improvement it would be if DADS all over the nation decided to just be more patient with their children. It is a choice, and it's our job to develop our children... to live intentionally with them, and not in a reactionary way. I think the effect of this on the hearts and minds of our children is profound.

The patience perspective is made up of three key parts:

A Thankful Heart

The first aspect in becoming more patient is to have a thankful heart. If anything happened to your son or daughter and they were not here anymore, you'd give anything to have them back. All of a sudden, them spilling something all over the floor, or bothering you when you're working on an important project slides into focus. Those disruptions are really not that important.

When we change our perspective and think of it that way, all the things that had us so upset and made us so short tempered don't matter one bit. Some can even be used as teachable moments instead of fits of rage.

Have those thoughts and those mental conversations with yourself before the impatience sets in. That way you've got things in proper perspective and your thankful heart takes over. Instead of being angry, you may find you become thankful your children are with you, healthy and happy.

Being patient with our children doesn't mean we don't correct them, and it doesn't mean we don't discipline them in order to show them a better way. It just means that before we allow ourselves to get so frustrated and so aggravated, and snap at them, we catch ourselves and turn it into a teachable moment.

There isn't a parent it in the entire world, whose child is in a cancer wing, who doesn't think about this. What would they give to take back any moment when they were impatient or angry towards their children?

A Slow Tongue

The same holds true with the slow tongue. Parents just don't realize just how damaging words can be when we criticize, demean, or speak harshly towards our children.

We have to be slow to respond, and we should not say things that are the opposite of the questions we must answer... those fundamental questions our children have in their hearts. We have to be so careful that we never say things that tell them the opposite. We can follow these simple guidelines: THINK before you speak.

T	Is it TRUE?
H	is it HELPFUL?
I	is it INSPIRING?
N	is it NECESSARY?
K	is it KIND?

A Good Memory

We need to have a good memory. Take a moment and search back to your own childhood. Try to remember what it was like when you were their age. It is important to think back and reconnect with what we were doing when we were the same age our children are now.

When your son does something really stupid, before you blow your stack, think back to what you were doing at that same age. Of course when you were eight years old you rarely showered, set traps for your little sister on the stairs, and left rocks in your pockets that damaged the washing machine. You know you wiped your boogers on the side of your bed, walked in the house with muddy shoes, and left the milk out. So here we are as DADS, getting all bent out of shape over the EXACT same things we did. We need to work on our memories!

I can't help but question some aspects of our public educational system here in the US. My biggest issue is with all the rules. I understand that order is important. I also understand that "Sit down, be quiet.", "Get in line.", "Don't touch that.", "Don't run.", and "No tackling on the playground," aren't habits that lead to success in life. It's the wrong message.

Kids are wired with very important success traits like curiosity, a sense of urgency, a positive attitude, and a hands-on approach to learning. If we are not careful, school can strip it right out of them. I think it is part of our job as DADS to foster those qualities at home, and that requires patience.

A woman observed a DAD in the grocery store with a three year old boy in his cart. As they passed the cookie section, the child asked for cookies and his father told him "no." The little boy immediately began to whine and fuss, and the DAD said quietly, "Now Tommy, we just have half of the aisles left to go through; don't be upset. It won't be long." She passed the DAD again in the candy aisle. Of course, the little boy began to shout for candy. When he was told he couldn't have any, he began to cry.

The DAD said, "There, there, Tommy, don't cry. Only two more aisles to go, and then we'll be checking out." The woman again happened to be behind the pair at the checkout, where the little boy immediately began to clamor for gum and burst into a terrible tantrum upon discovering there would be no gum purchased today.

The DAD patiently said, "Tommy, we'll be through this checkout lane in five minutes, and then you can go home and have a nice nap." The woman followed them out to the parking lot and stopped the man to compliment him. "I couldn't help noticing how patient you were with little Tommy..."

The DAD broke in, "My little boy's name is Joey ... **I'm** Tommy."

Hey, whatever it takes, DAD!

Patience is the companion of wisdom.
-Saint Augustine

Patience is bitter, but its fruit is sweet.
-Jean-Jacques Rousseau

Genius is nothing but a great aptitude for patience
-George-Loius De Buffon

A man who is a master of patience is a master of everything else.
-George Savile

How poor are they that have not patience! What wound did ever heal but by degrees?
-William Shakespeare

Patience is not passive. On the contrary, it is active, it is concentrated strength.
- Edward G. Bulwer-Lytton

"Learn the art of patience. Apply discipline to your thoughts when they become anxious over the outcome of a goal. Impatience breeds anxiety, fear, discouragement and failure. Patience creates confidence, decisiveness, and a rational outlook, which eventually leads to success.
-Brian Adams

Chapter Three

Serious DAD
Silly DAD

> "A merry heart does good like a medicine."
> **- Proverbs**

The idea that there are children who grow up without laughter in their home is a deeply disturbing thought. Laughter is critical to our development, and without it a child is robbed of their potential. Many emotionally wounded men cover their hurts by displaying a super-serious, "tough guy" image. It is simply a way they protect themselves from becoming wounded again. It most likely started when they were young kids or teens.

Some overly serious men are that way not because of past wounds, but because of massive responsibility or stress in their lives. Others may be struggling with a serious case of cynicism ("clinically cynical" as I like to call it) or negativity because life is not turning out the way they had hoped. Kids are born happy and full of joy and laughter, and then are taught to be negative, cynical and overly serious.

It is so important for you to be silly with your boys and girls. I live to make my daughter laugh. Her personality and sense of humor is exactly like mine, where as my younger son is more like my wife. I can make my daughter burst out laughing at a moment's notice, (and I constantly look for ways to do that) but it takes a little more work to get my son going… and I may very well only get a grin or a chuckle. I feel that my effort to make my kids laugh is equally as important as my efforts to teach them success principles and discipline.

The single most important thing for some of you DADS reading this book is to crank up the silly factor. Jack up your sweat pants to your arm pits and jump around the living room like a raving idiot. (Just make sure their friends aren't over) You will be amazed at the shrieks of delight you'll get, and they may even join in, depending on the music! The younger they are the easier it is.

I can't tell you how many times I have transferred joy from my heart to the hearts of my children by allowing myself to be silly and take myself back to being an 8 year old again. Try it. They will love you for it!

A few props to raise your silly score:

1. Clothes that are way too small
2. Clothes that are way too big
3. A massive afro wig (or any wig for that matter)
4. 70's music
5. Fake teeth

The Most Powerful Man In The World

One year for Christmas I bought everyone, including my niece and nephews, black teeth. We posed for the best Hillbilly family portrait ever!

Another reason why I feel that it is healthy for us to laugh with our sons and daughters is because of the very fact that life is tough. A good sense of humor, silliness, and laughter enable us to get through. Sometimes things are so frustrating all you can do is laugh. We've all been there. We also need to be able to laugh at ourselves. I am intentionally building this into our children. It's annoying to be around people who take themselves too seriously.

One time my son and I were fishing with a couple of friends and their young sons at a lake in Texas. Nate was about 6 or 7 years old, and at that age he was fairly inclined to ignore the advice of someone who is 32 years older, and who has extensively more experience standing at the edge of lakes.

So, of course, he eventually fell in.

As he pulled himself out and stepped back onto shore, the reality of the situation set in... his reality anyway. He was soaked, embarrassed, and the other boys were laughing hysterically. As he began to melt down and allow his emotions to lead him off into the woods and never return to civilization, I felt compelled to refocus him.

I said, "Hey Nate – two things:

#1: You are fine.
#2: It's funny when people fall in the lake."

That simple "refocus" headed off the meltdown, returned him to society, made him realize that there was no crisis. Best of all, it gave him permission to laugh at the next guy who falls in the lake. Many times, as we ride the emotional rapids of middle school and high school, the ability to laugh at ourselves can lessen the blow of insults and disarm the verbal bully. This is a skill well worth teaching our children.

So how do we balance this idea of silliness and laughter with the need to be serious at times? How do we let our kids know there is a need for order and discipline as well as humor? The "vibe" in our homes is the key. I do everything I can to make sure my home is one of peace and joy. So my goal is to create and protect that. At times that requires me to be serious, but the overall prevailing feelings should be peace and joy. Laughter sounds better to me than yelling. Let's make sure we are intentionally silly, and let's laugh with them as much as we can.

Another thing I have always thoroughly enjoyed is the art of telling my kids wildly untrue stories about my past. My favorite guilty pleasure is tricking and bamboozling my intelligent but gullible kids. I had my 5 year old convinced that I had the prestigious honor of being named the "cutest baby in the world" back in 1969. She also believed that I was the second place finisher in the World Chess Championships, losing only to the famed Wong Li, from China.

My son, at the age of 9, told his entire 3rd grade class that his grandfather's father was a Jedi, in the Navy. I had brought my DAD in on that scam just in case I was being questioned a little deeper. When I received the note from his teacher I decided to come clean.

The Most Powerful Man In The World

At 10, my son and I entered the hardware store on a mission. It was up to him, of course, to ask the kind gentleman in the apron where the "mozzarella seeds" could be found. It took several weeks of careful convincing before Nate fully bought into the idea that mozzarella cheese grows on trees, and that we would soon be in the cheese business. The older gentleman Nate asked caught my wink just in time, and directed us to aisle 33. There were only 32 aisles. Part of a father's job is to trick his trusting children!

The main things I need to be serious about are making sure no outside influences derail the most important things in my life; my marriage and children, prayer, work ethic, responsibility, respectful communication within the family, and how we treat other people. The truth is, 95% of the time these things can be done with a smile. You can be intense, with a smile. You can be tough, with a smile, and you can be focused, with a smile.

The Value of a Little Innocent Mischief

When dealing with our children I think it is important to let them know that a little bit of mischief is okay. Now of course I'm not talking about vandalism or behavior that hurts other people. I am referring to the fact that mischief is part of being a kid, and too often we forget that. I try to create situations where my children can have that experience. I tell them stories about when I was a kid and of the little things that we did that got us into a bit of trouble.

Looking back, I wish I had more fun when I was a kid. I was often bored, so I try to create situations where my kids can have a blast and have memories that will last a lifetime. One of my biggest regrets as a 43 year old man is that as a kid I never was involved in a full blown food fight!

Chris Royce

I wanted to include a story, written by my daughter, that illustrates my point. Here is her account of our Beluga Whale adventure.

A Day in the Windy City
-By Olivia Royce

We were on another one of our father-daughter weekends, and this time, we were in Chicago. For an eleven year old girl, being in a new city with my DAD was exciting and everything we did seemed like an adventure. Since it was November, I was dressed in several layers and DAD was wearing a long dress coat. We had waited at least an hour before we finally entered the Shedd Aquarium. Not being "animal people" ourselves we thought we would just take a quick look around at some of the fish, and maybe see the Beluga whale show that was featured on the outside banners.

As soon as we got in, we made a beeline for the entrance to the show. We were surprised when the usher told us that the show was sold out. DAD and I looked at each other. We were annoyed and frustrated. We started to walk away.

The stadium where the Beluga whales were performing was pretty big. It was set down lower than the rest of the aquarium with a few large pools. A big window in the front allowed plenty of light and the ceiling was all open. The only things that separated it from the rest of the aquarium were enormous, manmade cliffs on either side. Each cliff reached about 40 feet and they were rough and covered with fake trees, rocks, and shrubs. The stadium was clearly designed so that no one but the audience in the bleachers could see the live show.

DAD and I walked away discouraged, but still determined to make our trip worthwhile. A stairway on the opposite side of the cliff led down to a different part of the aquarium. I ran my hand down the rope that separated the crowd from the rocky cliff. I noticed that this side of the cliff was much less steep and it had plenty of foliage. We stopped for a moment on the steps to try to figure out where we were going next. DAD had a grin on his face as he glanced at the cliff behind us.

"Oli, what do you say we climb up there. I bet we could watch the whole show." With DAD being the jokester he was, I started to laugh. "No, I'm serious, why don't you climb up there and scope things out?" My heart started to beat faster when I realized that he wasn't kidding. I was excited.

Hesitantly I replied, "Okay... but what happens if we get caught?" "Worst case scenario; they throw us out of the aquarium." I broke into a big smile. Here was an adventure.

I quietly took off my furry coat and handed it to DAD. We waited for the traffic on the stairway to calm down, and with a couple of nervous glances, I stepped over the rope. There was no turning back now. Since there was still an occasional pedestrian walking by, I had to hurry. The trees and bushes blocked my view, but I made my way up the cliff. As I got more excited, I climbed faster. Before I reached the top, a tree branch snagged my purple t-shirt and ripped off the sleeve. I barely noticed. Finally, I popped my head up at the very top. I was about eye level with the people on the top bleachers, but I had the best seat in the house. I could see everything perfectly. With a smile, I made my way back down to DAD.

"The view is great!" I said. "Perfect, let's go!"

We waited for the coast to be clear again, and DAD stepped over the rope to join me. I led the way up the cliff as DAD held both of our coats. At the top, we laid on our bellies. The fake bushes at the top concealed our faces, but allowed us to see the entire show!

The Beluga whales were cool enough, but our "balcony seats" made the whole experience that much more fun.

Right before the show ended, we made our way back down the cliff and blended into the crowd. We didn't get caught! I made sure to keep myself composed as we left the crime scene. I was jumping up and down as soon as we got out of the building. I had a ripped shirt and messy hair, but I didn't care. DAD and I had just snuck into, or more like above, a Beluga whale show! We turned a disappointment into an adventure. To this day, I still have that ripped purple t-shirt. Not because it fits, but because it reminds me of the adventure that I had with DAD.

That story and the ripped t-shirt are the best souvenirs of that whole weekend. She told the story to her friends and she still has the shirt to this day! I think it's important as DADS that we create these scenarios for our kids, and create memories they will carry with them forever. Enjoy a little mischief together.

The Value of Physical Affection

Your children crave and need physical affection. There are many studies that prove this. Touch influences our ability to deal with stress and pain, to form close relationships with other people, and even to fight off disease. Children and adolescents, hospitalized for psychiatric problems, show remarkable reductions in anxiety levels and positive changes in attitude when they receive a brief daily back rub.

> **"We like to hop. We like to hop on top of pop."**
> -Dr. Seuss, 1963

There is also significant proof that physical affection increases happiness and self esteem, and decreases susceptibility to depression. It's common sense that being affectionate with your kids is a good thing. They have a need for you, DAD, to pick them up, hug & kiss them, hold their hands and wrestle with them. They need you to fall on the floor and let them jump all over you. Your son wants you to grab him in a playful head lock and give him a "noogie" or two!

When they are little they love to walk up your body as you hold their hands and then flip them over and swing them through your legs. You need to throw them on the couch into all the pillows, wrap them up in a blanket like a taco, and tickle them.

When my kids were small they would climb in bed with us every morning and snuggle up. That time passes way too fast. My daughter and I would watch Sesame Street every morning in bed. What pure joy for both of us. A few years later it was my son's turn to join us and the joy continued. As they grew older, the bed became a ship surrounded by alligators, sharks, and pirates. The pillows became rocks to step on in the carpet ocean, and the chair in the corner was the island they needed to land on before time ran out. Sometimes I would reach out and grab them and pull them aboard just in the nick of time. Other times I was the alligator or the shark nipping at their feet as they made their way back. As my daughter reached the age where jumping in bed with us was no longer appropriate, it freed up room for the bed to become a full-fledged wrestling arena for my son and me. Some epic battles have been waged there. Once you are off the bed, you lose. Landing on your head is an even more humiliating defeat.

A young boy desperately needs to test himself against the strength of his father. And we DADS need to walk the line between letting him win and frustrating him. I always make sure he gets his share of shots, pins and takedowns. It builds his confidence. I know there will be a day when he's letting me get mine.

I don't believe in using my hands in any way to inflict pain on my children. The extension of my hands should only represent love, affection, and comfort. If someone does get hurt when we are rough housing, I am quick to comfort.

Be affectionate with your kids, even if your DAD wasn't that way with you. You have the power to start now. Hold their hands. Let them crawl up on your lap. Give them high fives. Squeeze them tight. Cuddle them before bed. Rub their head and tell them how blessed you are to have them in your life.

The Most Powerful Man In The World

The Hillbilly Family Christmas

The Most Powerful Man In The World

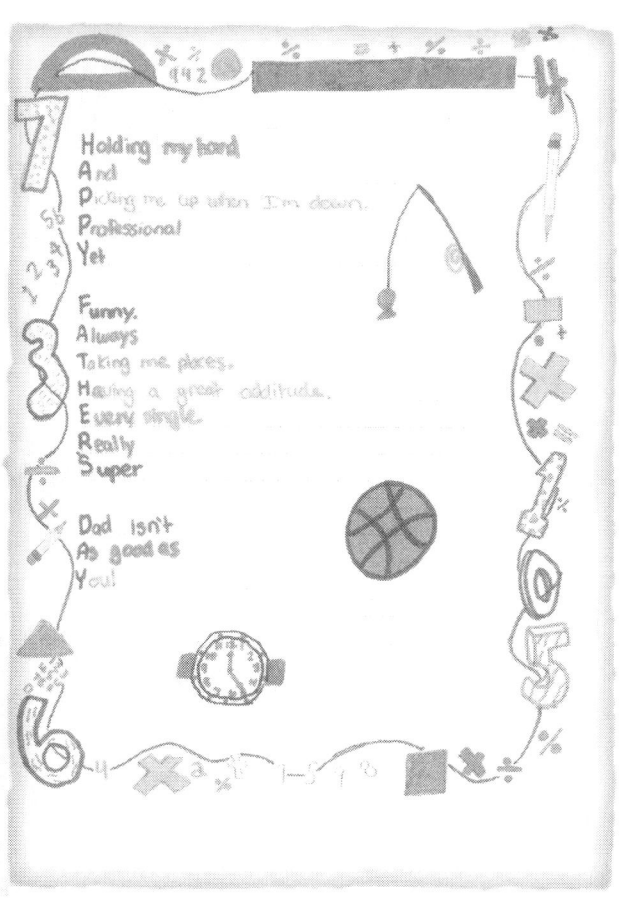

Chapter Four

Never, Always and The One Thing We Must Keep

As a world class DAD, we need to hold ourselves to world class standards. Here are a few simple but powerful standards that will make a huge difference in your lives. The level of quality or excellence we should try to live up to starts with our actions. Here is a list of guidelines and realizations that I hope will define the path worldclass DADS need to follow.

Words are incredibly powerful. The "sticks and stones" theory is dead wrong. Words can tear down or build up. Your words, DAD, are extra powerful in the lives of your sons and daughters.

"Life and death are in the power of the tongue."
– Proverbs

Life and death! In our modern day society words come cheap. They fly around the world at the speed of light, floating through the air in a billion giant twisted text messages. The internet is over loaded with idle words and useless trivial crap. We can separate ourselves from the masses very quickly by being intentional with our words. The things we say to our children matter, regardless how tired, frustrated, or angry we are. The way we talk to our wife matters. This is especially true when she is temporarily visiting another planet for 4 – 6 days a month, and especially when she is stressed and frazzled. This effort, to keep high standards when everyone around us is melting down, takes REAL strength and REAL manhood. I am challenged as I write this, believe me!

Here is a list of "Never and Always" that will serve us well, men!

1. **NEVER** criticize your daughter's appearance, especially when she is a teenager. Let mom deal with the pimples and the hair and the body issues. (Single DADS can get help from a loving, caring, older woman.)

2. **ALWAYS** tell her she is lovely. Greet her with, "Good morning beautiful!" That looks great. You look great. Wow, what a nice dress! Your hair looks fantastic. You look amazing!"

Some grown women cannot receive a genuine compliment because their father was critical, and picked them apart when they needed his affirmation the most. Don't be that kind of DAD.

3. **NEVER** tell your son he doesn't measure up, or he doesn't have what it takes. Don't say things like, "You are always in the way." "You never get it right." "You can't..."

This can also be done in a more covert way, rather than outright, so be careful. Make sure you don't undermine his growing masculinity by discouraging him, and don't let mom do it, either.

4. **ALWAYS** tell him he has what it takes. You believe in him, he can do it, he's courageous, he strong, he's able, he's a wild man.

5. **NEVER** make your love conditional on performance. Encourage peak performance, but never base your love or the way you treat them on their performance. This can be devastating to their future spouses.

6. **ALWAYS** tell them you are proud of them, and you love them. Breathe life into them by hugging them and kissing them and telling them you are so thankful they are yours! They are never too old for this!

7. **NEVER** tolerate complaining in your house. Complaining, from you, your wife, or your children will drag your family down. It is a trademark of the average and ordinary.

8. **ALWAYS** take full responsibility and talk about what can be done, instead of what can't be done.

9. **NEVER** allow name calling between any family members. EVER! And not between any kids that come over. Name calling has a devastating effect on respect in a relationship.

10. **ALWAYS** build each other up. It's powerful for the family to hear DAD only saying positive things to them. This way, when correction is necessary, they will listen.

11. **NEVER** hang up on each other. Hanging up the phone on someone should be unacceptable. Finish a conversation and end on a positive note.

12. **NEVER** go to bed mad. This one is tough, guys, but well worth the effort. We've spent many a late night hashing things out just to keep our standard of "not letting the sun go down on our wrath." So many arguments, fights and misunderstandings needlessly carry over to the next day (or days!), when they could've just been worked out before bed.

13. **ALWAYS** forgive. It can be the hardest *and* easiest thing to do.

14. **NEVER** lie.

15. **ALWAYS** tell the truth. They are both choices.

16. **ALWAYS** keep your word.

Wow. What a difference a man can make by simply doing what he says he will do. I just can't believe how rare it is today. I see people who wonder why they lack results in their lives, but they never keep their word. It's painfully obvious why they are frustrated and nothing changes. Whatever happened to yes is yes and no is no?

Our kids need to be able to count on us. We all over commit, and yes, our intentions are usually good, but when we DADS say we are going to do something, we damn well better do it. The world and other people will let our kids down enough; they don't need it from us! I am so glad I have had the opportunity to be around world class men who keep their word, and will call you out when you don't.

I had a life altering situation happen to me in 2004. Early on in the year I was visiting a gentleman named Mike at his home in Dallas, Texas. I had flown in to see him for two days because I wanted to gain insight into how he had become so successful. He is a very wealthy businessman, but it was the other aspects of his life that I was particularly interested in. He is known for his generosity, creative giving, and ability to build relationships.

In his office he had several fish mounts of Peacock Bass he'd caught in the Amazon River, in Brazil. In my excitement, I said to him, "Wow, these are cool, I read about these Amazon adventures, and I've always wanted to go!"

His casual reply was, "OK, I'll put you on the list." Nothing else was said.

Several months later, I was in California on a business trip when I received a call on my cell phone. It was Mike. He said, "Are you all set for the Amazon?" My response was just like every average, ordinary, non committal, word breaking man. "Oh, well, uh, I don't think I will be able to make it. When are the dates again? (The trip was 2 months later, in October) I have a family vacation in October to Disney."

His reply changed my life. He said, "Whoa, wait a minute. You never said you *weren't* going." How's that for a different perspective? But wait, it gets better. He said, "I put you on the list. I reserved a spot for you that could've gone to someone else. Now my word is on the line. Am I supposed to tell these guys we are one short just because you can't get your schedule straight?" How's that for getting called out?

I said, "Mike, I am in California – give me 24 hours to get home to NY, and I will call you back tomorrow." I immediately called my wife. "Sherri, we have an issue." When I told her about the situation, her response was amazing. She simply said, "Well, we gotta do what we gotta do. Your reputation with Mike is worth way more than whatever we have to do."

Wow! What a cool wife.

When I returned home, I called Mike and said, "I'm in. I'll be there." I wrote a check for $5,000 for the trip, applied for my Brazilian Tourist VISA, ordered my equipment, and got my shots. As it turned out, the family vacation ended the day the fishing trip started. After 9 days in Disney, my family flew back to Syracuse, NY and I hopped on a plane to Miami, Florida. I met up with Mike then headed to Brazil for 9 more days on the river. It was the trip of a lifetime.

I had reached an "Aha" moment when I decided I was going to keep my word, no matter what the cost! Something shifted that day, and I separated myself from the countless other men that think it is OK to say one thing and do another. The greatest lesson I learned was that if I am going to play at the world class level, I am going to have to keep my word. Yes is yes and no is no. "Maybe" doesn't exist in the vocabulary of the world class. It's a useless word that really means, "No, but I don't have the balls to tell you no right now."

I will always be grateful to Mike, and Sherri, for helping me grow and become a better man.

We need to keep our word with our sons and daughters. We just can't tell them, "Yes, I will play catch with you", and then blow it off because we are tired, or because the game went into overtime. We need to consider our commitments before we make them, and once we make them, fight to keep them.

The Most Powerful Man In The World

The Amazon River in Brazil is the best place on earth for big Peacock Bass! You should go...

The Most Powerful Man In The World

> "It's Easier To Build Strong Children Than To Repair Broken Men."
>
> -Frederick Douglass

Chapter Five

Fight For Their Hearts

Think of all that competes for a piece of our children's hearts. TV. Music. The Internet. Texting. YOUTUBE. Facebook. Twitter. Mario. Halo. Madden. Harry Potter. Twilight. Friends. Sports. Clubs. Activities. WOW! Where do **WE** fit in?

None of these things, in and of themselves, are capable of stealing their hearts. They don't have any more power than what we give them. If we don't have a plan, however, and we are not intentional about fighting for their hearts, the collective assault will prevail.

I didn't even mention the insidious and evil things that can really cause damage to a child's or teenager's heart. There is alcohol, drugs, pornography, divorce, abortion, abuse, eating disorders, depression... just to name a few. This world is dangerous. The war between good and evil has raged for thousands of years, and it seems to be escalating.

As DADS, we cannot afford to be naive. We must be on-guard and stay connected.

I want to give you some of the things we have done to fight for our children's hearts. Some activities are very simple, others require more effort. Some are absolutely free, others require resources. You need to figure out what your resources will allow and what's right for your family. What we have tried has been effective, and has brought me great joy.

1. **HANDLE WITH CARE**

Remember in the "Christmas Story", when Ralphy's DAD received his "major award"? He read the word on the crate… "FRA – GEEL – A" (FRAGILE) Well, our children's hearts can be FRA-GEEL-A. They must be handled with extreme care.

When we talk to them we must remember their questions. (I covered them in the previous chapter "Answer Their Questions.") When we discipline them, we are actually fighting for their hearts, if we are doing it out of love and not anger. If their future is on our mind and not how we feel at the moment, we can help them make better decisions.

The ultimate objective is that they make good choices- not to avoid punishment, but because it's the wisest thing to do. Not disappointing my wife and me is a better motivator for our children than not getting caught.

When my son was 10 he looked at something on YouTube that he shouldn't have. We had agreed that there would be no downloading any videos unless his mom or I approved it first, as a way to protect him.

The Most Powerful Man In The World

One evening my wife called him for dinner, and when he didn't come right away, her mom sense kicked in and she knew he was up to something he shouldn't be. When she questioned him, he wasn't honest with her. Man, is it disappointing when our children don't tell the truth. He said he was watching a comedian on YouTube that his buddy told him about.

Even though she knew he was lying, she was wise enough to let it play out instead of getting in his face. I was out of town at the time. The next day the guilt was weighing on him so much he went to his Mom and confessed that he had lied. His reason was he did not want to jeopardize his movie date with her. He thought she would have pulled the plug on it. When he came clean he told her that he had watched a video of "a girl dancing in her underwear."

When I came home two days later, my son said he needed to talk to me. He told me that he had not been the man of the house when I was gone. He said that he had lied to his mother, and that he watched a video that he shouldn't have. As I listened, I realized that this was a tremendous opportunity to fight for my son's heart, and for our relationship to be strengthened. This was not a time to be angry, condemning, or harsh with him. My 10 year old boy had been tempted. He made two very wrong decisions... one in the name of curiosity, and the other was lying to get something he wanted – a movie night.

First we discussed trust and honesty. Lying to us is unacceptable, and it only leads to more pain and disappointment. Second, we discussed how important it is to guard what we allow ourselves to see and hear. This opened up our dialogue on pornography. I told him that on average most boys are first exposed to pornography by age 10. This can affect boys as they grow into men. We need to stand guard, and they want us to. We promised each other we would face these things together. We prayed together for strength and wisdom, and our relationship became stronger as father and son.

2. SAFE ZONES

Every family is going to have their squabbles, arguments, conflicts- basic family strife. We are going to be tired and stressed at times. The kids will argue and get after each other. Some degree of strife is inevitable.

We have instituted a concept called "SAFE ZONES" to help protect the environment in our home and protect our family. These are times where everyone is on high alert against strife. Anyone can remind the rest of us that such behavior is unacceptable during these times. We have four.

Before school
Before bed
Vacations
Friday night family night

I feel very strongly about leaving the house peacefully, always on good terms. I don't believe that our kids should head off to school upset, and there should be no yelling first thing in the morning. It's a high priority. The same holds true before bed. Too many kids cry themselves to sleep. What a tragedy! DAD – your kids should fall asleep peacefully knowing everything is fine and tomorrow will be a great day of promise.

Have you ever had a vacation ruined by an argument? That's the memory you all take home – Mom and DAD'S "big fight"? Which means you paid money to go somewhere to yell at each other! How dumb. We've been fortunate to have many great family vacations. All of which are documented on the "Wall of Trips" in our home. The photos from each trip are narrowed down to the top 8 pictures that show what we did. There are currently 23 frames on display to remind all of us how special our time is together.

We learned this important lesson after a trip to Jamaica, which was over shadowed by my wife and I getting into a fight over nothing. We decided to make sure no family vacation would ever be ruined by strife. We've been on guard ever since!

3. DEDICATED FAMILY NIGHT

When I started my business back in 1999, my daughter was an infant. I knew I would have to jump in with both feet and work hard if I was going be successful. I was OK with that. I also knew I did not want to neglect my family. This can be a tricky proposition. We established two times during the week that were dedicated family times. Friday night has been a great time that we all look forward to throughout the week. I have also chosen not to work on Sundays.

This family time must be protected. It is also a safe zone against strife. It must be protected against anything that might detract from it, which, for us, includes friends and other family members outside the immediate family. Very rarely do we veer off our game plan on a Friday night. I am aware that, as kids get older, there is more to do on Fridays. Eventually you will be facing a balancing act because you want them to participate but you don't want them to resent the family night.

Each family will have to figure out what works for them. One tip that I have is to make sure you do things that are really fun, and put in the effort to make it attractive. You may be tired, DAD, but you'll have to push through. It's worth it. Just declaring it isn't enough. You'll need to get creative with what you're going to do. Talking about it during the week helps and it gives everyone something to look forward to.

Have the kids give you their ideas, and here are a few of ours: Set up competitions. Choose 4 or 5 events that are different...each one may favor different family member's skills or strengths. Set up a point system, and the winner chooses the movie for the night. Let each member choose the type of food/recipes and make an ethnic dinner together. Have a campfire and tell your kids stories of your adventures when you were their age!

There are a million things you can go and do together that are unique to where you live. Do some research and put in the time. Your family will be thrilled you have set aside the time for them. Put away the IPods and IPads and IPhones, and love up on the most important people in your life.

4. BIG ADVENTURES!

The younger your son is, the easier this is. And of course you can do these things with your daughters!

When my son was a little guy I realized that a major desire (even need) of the male gender is adventure. It becomes evident at a very young age. As far back as I can remember he was always clutching a stick, or a rock, or some kind of "weapon". I would say to him, "Hey, Nate – let's go on a big adventure!" He would get so excited he could hardly stand it. Then he began to gather up the essential items he figured we would need, and load up his Spiderman backpack with:

        1 Plastic gun with broken tip
        1 Pair of red wristbands
        1 Flashlight
        2 Packages of Keebler crackers and cheese
        2 Juice boxes
        1 Screwdriver
        1 Sack of marbles
        1 Lego spaceship

Now we were ready. Off we went. The younger they are the closer to the house you can stay. Any patch of woods, even the one at the end of your street, serves as the great wilderness expedition of the day! Oddly enough, the success of our excursions came to be judged by how many scratches we came home with. The pricker bushes provided proof of our bravado, I guess.

As my son got older, the outward radius from our house increased and the items he packed changed to:

        2 Walkie talkies
        1 Sling shot
        1 Bag of beef jerky
        2 Bottled waters
        2 Walking sticks
        1 Survival knife with matches

However, the excitement and the joy was still there. We've taken a couple of his buddies with us, and sadly to say, it was their first time on an adventure hike. Here's an idea that your 4 – 7 yr. old son/daughter will absolutely love:

Chris Royce

The Treasure Map

Get a bag of coins, preferably silver dollars and quarters, and some costume jewelry that looks like treasure. Bury it in the woods somewhere... under a fallen tree or by an old stump.

Now get a large brown paper grocery bag and open it up. Grab a sharpie and draw out a treasure map. Include the key land marks. Make it look "piratey"! So what if you failed art class 100 years ago in high school. Add some color if you want. Crumple it up a bunch of times so it gets soft and looks old. Then take a lighter and burn the edges and a few small holes here and there. Now roll it up and put a small piece of rawhide or string around it.

Craft a story about how you ended up with this ancient treasure map, gather your supplies, and get after it. PURE JOY! He'll never forget it. His friends will be incredibly jealous, and you're the hero, DAD!

5. BUILD A ROBOT!!

Start your search for the best boxes, scrap pieces of duct work, shiny things, and random robot parts! Stock up on duct tape, spray glue, and staples. Spray paint is cheap and comes in a million colors, including silver and gold! Collecting all the pieces and parts is half the fun. Building it and blowing it up is the other half!

The first time my son and I did this was a great learning experience for me. Nate was about 6 or 7 years old, and he could hardly contain himself at my suggestion of building a robot. He had visions, of course, of a fully functioning missile launching apparatus with lasers that could talk. He even mentioned that he wanted it to have hands that "could come down and make sandwiches." I assured him we could probably figure out the missiles and lasers, but the human like behaviors would not be part of this prototype.

I am not handy. Fixing things, let alone building them, is not one of my gifts. You DADS that are handy or skilled are going to be able to build some very cool robots. Ours have been more in the category of "interesting".

So, we collected the pieces and parts over a month or two, and we set aside a Sunday afternoon for the official build. We were excited! The various sized boxes stacked on each other formed a nice 4' body. Old corrugated ductwork made great arms. We mounted plastic water bottles on the sides for the missile launchers – perfect size for the bottle rockets that would be our missiles. Shoe boxes became feet. Silver spray paint, duct tape and a couple soda cans for eyes finished him off.

The day we chose was a bit rainy, so we decided to place the "Bot" facing outward from the garage. That way we could launch the bottle rockets. (Towards the neighbor's house) That day I learned 5 important lessons:

#1. The temperature at which a bottle rocket ignites and burns before it launches greatly exceeds the temperature at which a plastic water bottle melts.

#2. When a plastic bottle attached to a cardboard box begins to melt, it burns through the aforementioned cardboard box and falls inside the box.

#3. When a flaming bottle rocket launches inside a cardboard box, it causes the box to burst into flames.

#4. A flaming cardboard robot must not be allowed to remain in a garage.

#5. When your father – son robot goes up in a flaming inferno, and your son watches you repeatedly kick it out of the garage and into the rain, he cries.

Well, we had fun building it anyway. (Our engineering department needed to be revamped, that's all.)

Your son will so much appreciate the time together. Get creative. Carve out the time, and take pictures of your creation before it goes up in flames!

The Most Powerful Man In The World

My son wanted you to have the official blueprints, so here they are:

How to Make a regular cardboard box robot

- First, you have to get together a bunch of cardboard boxes and other cardboard things you might need.

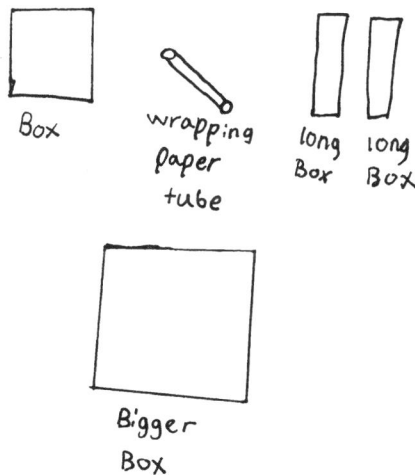

Box • wrapping paper tube • long Box • long Box

Bigger Box

- Second, get ducttape, Markers, spray paint any colors, and scissors

  O 🖉🖉 ◊ ✂

- Third, you duct tape the little box to the bigger box

  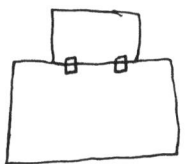

- Fourth, cut two holes in the sides of the bigger box even with each other

The Most Powerful Man In The World

- Fifth, Put the wrapping paper tube in the holes and secure with ducttape

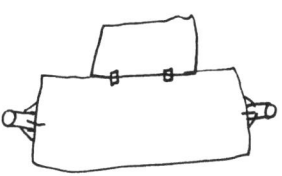

- Sixth, ducttape the two long boxes to the bigger box

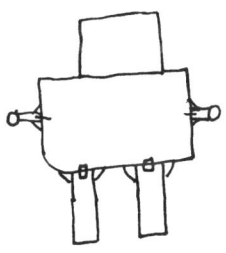

Chris Royce

- Seventh, decorate with the spray paint and markers and anything else shiny and cool.

and now you have a awsome robot!

6. FORTS & TREE HOUSES:

For those of you who can build things, a tree house or some type of fort in the woods is a total hit. One year I flew my DAD up from North Carolina to build a tree house for the kids. A close friend of mine, Lou Gonzales, who is an amazing problem solver and super handy builder, generously lent his talents. (My role was handing them things.) They built an incredibly cool structure that ultimately became known as "The Flying Dutchman."

7. WALKING STICKS/SPEARS

We've enjoyed searching for the perfect saplings… the right height, thickness and density. Once we find a couple, we'll peel off the bark and use our pocket knives to chip away at the bumps and knots. We use sand paper to make them super smooth and then spray them with polyurethane. Once the walking sticks are finished, we add the finishing touch. An Indian arrowhead inserted into a notch we cut in the top. (A little super glue helps!) For the final detail we wrap the top 3 or 4 inches with thin rope or twine and glue that down. There you have it – matching father/son spears ready for your next adventure in the woods!

8. BOW AND ARROWS

We have never advanced to this level in homemade weaponry, however a close friend of mine and his son have. Mark Edwards and his son, Asher, have constructed some very cool bows and arrows together. Mark has told me how much his son (who was 9 at the time) enjoyed that special time, and how much he got into the project.

9. CRITTER CATCHING

Hunting for things that crawl, creep or slither is pure joy for most boys, and some girls. (Only the really cool ones!) It is a fantastic investment of time to set aside an afternoon and "head upstream". Find a stream you can both walk in, or along, and start flipping some rocks. My DAD did this with me, and I still remember it 35 years later as one of our most enjoyable times together. Just grab a small net and a couple coffee cans with holes in the lids, and start scooping up critters. Crayfish, salamanders, mud puppies, small fish, bugs... you name it! You can get an Audubon Society Field Guide for about $10 if you want to identify what you're catching... or to avoid the poisonous things.

If you want to take it up a notch, for around $300 you can get yourselves a very nice laboratory quality microscope. This opens up a whole new world of creepy discovery. You can now see bugs on the bugs! We've had all the kids in the neighborhood lined up to look at the crazy things we've caught. It's great to gather your specimens in baby food jars and save them for a rainy day. Then instead of watching TV, bust out the microscope and see what you can see!

10. PLAY ARMY MEN!

Remember the classic army men? I'm talking about the real deal vintage ones, not the dollar store cheesy crap ones that the heads fall off. The originals from the 60's and 70's were made with quality. There is the laying – down guy, the bazooka guy, the metal detector guy, the grenade tossing guy, and the radio guy, to name a few of the ones we all remember! The simple version of our army men game is this:

1. Count out 15 or 20 men each.
2. Set up your formation on opposite ends of the room or hallway, at least 10' apart.
3. Get your rubber bands ready!
4. You get 10 shots each, alternating.
5. Count your kills.
6. The winner keeps the flag until next time.

The Most Powerful Man In The World

I am amazed at how much fun this is for my son and me. It's really about the time, and being on the floor together. Getting down to your young son's level and playing with him with enthusiasm is absolutely critical. So what if you're tired. So what if your DAD didn't do it with you. Do it while you can.

I was speaking to a group of about 150 men at a Band of Brothers Boot camp in California and I was talking to them about this simple idea - of playing army men with their sons. After the event, a man came up to me with tears in his eyes, and said, "My son is 15, and he just put away his army men… I never played them with him. I am going to go home and ask him to get them out so we can play."

I simply said, "What a great idea. He'll be more than willing to do that, I'm sure!"

11. FATHER/DAUGHTER AND FATHER/SON WEEKENDS

When my daughter turned 10 we went on our first annual Father/Daughter weekend. What an impact this had on our relationship! We spent three days and two nights in NYC.

We watched a Tony Award winning musical on Broadway, we dined at Tavern on the Green, we checked out 5th Avenue, we took a carriage ride though Central Park, and we took as many forms of transportation as we could, including a rick-shaw and a limo!

But you want to know the best part of all… the absolute highlight of the weekend? We held hands for three days straight. It was just Olivia and her daddy. WOW. Now that speaks loudly and says "You're lovely, and I see you!" We've since gone on several Father/Daughter weekends and trips, including Chicago, Raleigh, Niagara Falls, and the Dominican

Republic.

When my son turned 10 we headed off on our first Father/Son weekend. We went to see gramps in North Carolina. But it wasn't just a trip to visit grandpa; it was a double-triple header! We set up 6 things to do in 3 days.

> Zip lining
> Zoo
> Flea Market
> Fishing
> Movies (The 3 Stooges!)
> The National Ping Pong Championships for the Olympic Qualifiers

What a weekend! A high point for me was the flea market. I believe that we should teach our kids to negotiate at a young age. This is a skill that will serve them well in life regardless of what they go on to do, and there is no better venue for practice than the flea market! I gave Nate five $10 bills, and the rule was he could buy anything he wanted, however he couldn't pay full price. He had to negotiate the price down. He walked away with the following list of treasures, all at a discount:

> 1 Bag of vintage army men   ($4)
> 1 Telescopic magnet thingy   ($3)
> 4 Authentic Sioux arrowheads   ($12)
> 1 Package of bungee cords   ($6)
> 1 Mini clip on flashlight   ($3)

Not a bad take for a 10 year old. When we went to Boston on our next adventure, we focused on museums, American history, and how to travel and find your way around. I spent time teaching him how to pay attention to his surroundings and ride the trains. He came face to face with his first crack head on the subway. That was a bit disturbing for him and opened up a good discussion for us.

See, DAD, your kids need you to teach them about life. You have great value because of the sum total of your experiences. You have wisdom, insight and perspective. It's up to you to transfer it to them. The father- son and father-daughter weekends are a great way to do that.

12. THE ROYCE FAMILY SURPRISE WEEKENDS

I was bored a lot as a kid. My mom didn't like to travel much, or veer too far from her routine. I am just not wired that way. I gravitate towards travel, adventure, and surprises. Several years ago my wife and I came up with an idea. We thought it would be great if we planned an entire surprise weekend for the kids.

We schemed and planned and snuck around to get it all set up. Early on a Friday morning we woke the kids up and said, "Hurry hurry, get up! It's the first annual Royce Family Surprise weekend! Get dressed, were leaving in 30 minutes!"

> "Where are we going!?" they asked.
> "We are not at liberty to give you that information at this time," was our answer.

We repeated that at least 20 times before 9:00! We jumped in the car; bags pre-packed the night before, of course, and headed to the train station. From there, we headed downstate to NYC for a jam packed weekend of pure fun and excitement. The Times Square Hilton, the double-decker bus, the wax museum, Shrek on Broadway, Central Park, FAO Schwartz, Little Italy, and the Museum of Natural History were all conquered that weekend. They never knew what was next!

The second year we felt the need to outdo ourselves and make it an even bigger surprise. When they woke up Friday morning they thought they would be in school that afternoon, (skipping school is one of the best parts) however they found themselves on the way to Disney World instead! We were on a mad mission to Florida for the weekend. When we left, they began asking questions, and of course we refused to answer.

It wasn't until we hit the gate at our connecting airport and our daughter read ORLANDO on the sign that the freaking out began. It's so great to be able to do that for your children.

We also realized that as they caught on our plans had to be trickier and more covert. The third year we let them go to school, and then picked them up shortly after. For that trip we headed to a cabin in the Adirondacks.

We've since done other trips and what great memories we all have, and what a great way to fight for their hearts!

13. THE SUNDAY NIGHT FAMILY MEETING

I can't begin to tell you what a difference this has made for our family. But I'll try. We established that on Sunday evenings, after we eat dinner, we clear the table, sit back down together and we go over the prior week and the upcoming week. The approach is that we first discuss the victories and great things that happened the week before. We talk about the ground we are gaining in our lives.

Then we discuss our goals and responsibilities for the upcoming week. We take time to listen to what is on each other's plate. Then we pray. We start by thanking God for all He has done in our lives and for how He has come through for us throughout the past week. We pray for each other and what we all have to do. I have grown to depend on this special time together.

I find it no coincidence that many times right before we get ready to do it a potential argument, or strife, tries to work its way in, and distract us. It is hard to do this together if you are mad at each other. Conversely, it is absolutely amazing how much this can draw you closer to each other. The communication aspect is critical, and the prayer aspect is powerful. Give it a try for a few weeks, and see how you all feel. Take the lead, DAD!

Fighting for the hearts of your children is on you, DAD. There are so many ways you can do it. I have shared with you only a few. I am sure you are already doing many great things to create memories that will last a lifetime. It can be something inexpensive and simple, or elaborate and well planned. You get to choose. But make the choice for your children, your wife and your family. Just make sure that nothing else fights harder for their hearts than you do!

Chris Royce

Ready, Aim, Fire!

The new improved XJ VII model.

The Most Powerful Man In The World

Our 1st Father/Daughter Weekend in NYC. Here we are on Broadway. What a weekend we had!

If you want to fight for your daughter's heart take her on a carriage ride in Central Park.

Chris Royce

Father/Son Weekend, Ziplining in North Carolina.

If you want to practice patience, teach your little guy to fish.

The Most Powerful Man In The World

Our 1st Royce Family Surprise Weekend... getting some tats!

Like Father, Like Son? (That's not really me in the photo)

Chris Royce

Father/Daughter Weekend #4...
They grow up quick!

The Most Powerful Man In The World

2nd Annual Royce Family Surpirse Weekend, in Orlando.

Family Vacation in Jamaica

Chris Royce

Father/Daughter trip to Dominican Republic in 2010

*Royce Family Surprise Weekend #3
Adirondack Mountains, Upstate NY*

The Most Powerful Man In The World

Nate loves his Momma!

The kids getting ready to cheer on the Syracuse Orange.

Chris Royce

DAD- Your family just wants to spend time with you!

The Most Powerful Man In The World

August 12, 2016

Dear Dad,

    I just wanted to thank you with all of my heart for everything you do. I don't want this to be a lame "thank you" letter though.

    In my perspective, we are pretty much excactly alike in almost every way! That's really special. I had such a great time in the Dominican Republic not only because of the experiences, but because the trip brought us closer together and we "understood" each other the whole time!

    You've been able to help me through so many tough times. Everything from when I don't feel well, to when I'm about to go up on stage. Now I've realized (with the new things you've been able to help me with) that I can go to you for _anything_! Mostly this is because you know where I'm coming from!

    I think that we can be an inspiration to so many people if we really build our relationship! Here comes the <u>Royce Team</u>.

Thank you and You're the BEST!

Love,
Olivia

Chris Royce

Me And Dad List

Typed	Handwritten
Watch Star Wars	Wih Stre Wosret
Build A Robot	BiD A roBot
Build w/Legos	BiLB Winl tgo
Watch B-Ball Game w/Dad	Wih BE Ball Game Wir DAD
Wrestle	AnJ ACL
Play War of the Monsters	PLye WOkre fo the MOstr
Read a comic book	reJ a kk k Mik Book

Chapter Six

The 8x18 Factor

One of the crowning jewels of being a DAD is for our children to be successful in life. That means different things to all of us. It could be finding their calling, building wealth, helping people, becoming educated or raising a thriving family of their own. Whatever it is, I believe that it is up to us to intentionally impart key character traits to them.

What is your plan, DAD, to give your sons and daughters an edge in life?

Do we learn how to become successful in school? Is it even up to the public school system to teach our children how to win in life? Why aren't more practical life skills taught in school? I know we have some great teachers who love teaching and impacting our youth. I also know that we have plenty of teachers and administrators that don't have a clue. Curriculum is lacking when it comes to actual real world life skills. If it were up to me the class list would look a bit different. Here is my public school curriculum for truly equipping children for life:

Let's keep Math, English, Social Studies (with a stronger emphasis on American History and the Principles of the Founding Fathers), Sciences, Technology, Foreign Language (beginning in elementary school) and Health.

But let's add as mandatory classes: Goal setting, Time Management, Positive Thinking, Kindness 101, Conflict Resolution, Communication Skills, Personality Styles & People Skills, How Money Works (the actual truth), Marriage and Family, Entrepreneurship & Business, First Aid and CPR, Swimming, Self Defense, Drivers Ed, and Travel Safety.

Imagine if our public school system embraced this approach and young children all over the country were being taught these principles and skills. The teachers would make even more of an impact, and more children would stay in school. The good news is that you, DAD, can model and teach these at home.

As a foundation, I have **8 key traits** I believe make a huge difference in overall quality of life. If we have demonstrated and communicated these to our children by the age of 18, we've done well!

1. **Personal Responsibility**
2. **Honesty**
3. **Courage**
4. **Self Defense**
5. **Kindness**
6. **Humility**
7. **A Competitive Spirit**
8. **A Strong Work Ethic**

The Most Powerful Man In The World

When my son was very young (2-4 years old) I would tuck him into bed at night and tell him stories. All kids love stories! I made up a character, and I would use this character to teach my son principles about life. Grizzy Griz was a young bear who lived with his parents in a cave in the woods.

Typical, I guess. Now I made these stories up as I went along, but they sure held his attention. It gave me a way to talk about obeying your parents, honesty, courage, and other important character traits my son would need as a young boy and later on as a man. Looking back, I realized how much he relished these stories and that time together.

As our kids grow older, simple stories will need to change into more tangible demonstrations and opportunities to walk out the principles you are teaching them.

#1. Personal Responsibility

I have never met a successful person who has not taken 100% personal responsibility for their life. The younger we are when understanding this principle, the better. I finally got it at age 28. My life began to change almost immediately.

When a person takes 100% responsibility for their choices, it becomes unacceptable to complain, blame, or have self pity. Imagine the advantage a teenager who knows and understands this would have over his or her peers. Imagine a young adult entering the workforce with this attitude, and the difference his or her employer would see. They would have a clear edge in the marketplace.

All success, regardless of the realm in which it reveals itself, begins with accepting full responsibility.

As DADS who are serious about raising successful children, we must make sure they never hear us complain about our circumstances, or blame others. They should hear us talk positively about our life, our work, our wife, and the world. The news contains enough negativity for all of us. (It's not watched in my home.) Our homes need to be sanctuaries from the world, not reflections of it.

Do not allow them, regardless of their age, to make excuses. Do not tolerate them blaming their siblings for their mishaps. Set the bar high when it comes to complaining. The other day my son complained about being bored. The result: two hours of pulling weeds. The lesson: complaining doesn't get you what you want. (A thankful heart and good ideas supported by work gets you what you want.) It's up to us to teach them personal responsibility.

#2. Honesty

Honesty is defined as honor, straightforwardness, truthfulness, morality, goodness and justice.

I remember exactly where I was when I made the irrevocable decision that I wasn't going to lie again. I was in college, and I was 21 years old. I was tired of the effort it took to figure out who knew what, and who I told this or that. I guess I just realized how wrong and harmful it is. Twenty-one isn't that young to figure it out, but some of you reading this book haven't made that decision yet, and you're much older than that. If trust is the foundation of any strong and meaningful relationship, then honesty is the mortar in that foundation. In the 20 years of being with my wife, I have never lied to her. That's just a decision.

Remember, DAD, the best way we can give these life changing traits to our children is by modeling them. It's a much clearer message.

Be honest with your wife. Be honest with your kids. Be honest at work, or in your business. Then you can expect it from them, and it will serve them well in a dishonest world.

#3. Courage

"We shall not flag or fail. We shall go on to the end. We shall fight in France, we shall fight on the seas and the oceans, we shall fight with growing confidence and growing strength in the air, we shall defend our island, whatever the cost may be. We shall fight on the beaches, we shall fight on the landing grounds, we shall fight in the fields and in the streets, we shall fight in the hills; we shall never surrender."

-Winston Churchill

Messenger Boy: "The Thessalonian you're fighting... he's the biggest man I've ever seen. I wouldn't want to fight him."
Achilles: "That's why no one will remember your name."

-From the movie Troy

Why do these quotes stir something in us so deeply? It's because we as men so desperately want to be strong. We want to be taken seriously, and we want to show that we have a courageous heart. You do.

"Feel the fear and do it anyway." - unknown

A courageous heart and demonstrating courage in our lives does not mean we do not feel fearful. It means we go for it anyway. I was afraid to go into business, but I did it anyway. I was afraid to speak in front of people, but I did it anyway. I was afraid to write this book, but I did it anyway, as well as a million other things. Your kids need to see you step forward in the face of fear. It's OK for them to know we are afraid at times; it's not OK for us to allow them to be afraid and not face it. (With our help.)

One of the 3 things that my kids got paid for was to overcome fears. I wanted my children to get paid for the same things you get paid for in the real world, so we paid them for these things. (I will discuss the other two in a later chapter.) In my business life, I earned a significant amount of money for overcoming my own fears and discomforts.

One time we were at Disney's Hollywood Studios, waiting in line for the famed Tower of Terror, when the fear began to set in on my 6 year old daughter. The screams and the general vibe began to take its toll as we got closer to the tower. As the tears welled up, I had a decision to make. Was I going to let her off the hook, or was I going to coach her on the idea of courage? As we walked we discussed this opportunity to demonstrate courage in the face of fear, *and* the opportunity to earn 5 bucks. The tears were wiped away and she dug deep. (Deep into my forearm, that is!) The overpriced photo in the cardboard frame revealed the outcome... pure joy and the satisfaction of pushing past the fear, and being $5 richer.

I realize that many times the need for courage is much more serious than a ride at Disney. These opportunities, however, lay a foundation that can be built upon as they get older.

When my daughter was 12, she was going for her Black Belt. She had already been taking martial arts for 3 ½ years at that point, and one of the Black Belt requirements was to run 2 miles in under 16 minutes, 2 Saturdays in a row. It was January, and as long as the temperature was above 0, they would run. (Upstate New York!) For weeks she attempted to meet this final requirement, and for weeks she fell short. 16:15 & 16:05... painfully close. The weather was brutal, just 2 or 3 degrees above 0, with ice on the road and side walk. Many times, just yards before the finish line she would have to stop and get sick, adding seconds to her time that would put her over the 16 minutes. This went on for 6 weeks. As the deadline approached she began to worry that she wasn't going to be able to do it. That would mean pushing off the promotion for another 6 months. Unacceptable.

We focused on the courage she would need to make this happen. I drew from a promise in the Bible that I have used for myself many times to muster up the courage to move forward. **"I have not given you a spirit of fear, but one of power, love and a sound mind." 2 Timothy 1:7**

The world could use a bit more power, love and a few more sound minds! Olivia and I talked about this. We prayed together. She repeated the verse out loud as she prepared to run, and as she ran. We took her to an indoor track to help her get an image in her head of beating the time, which replaced a failure memory with a victory memory. As she headed into the final two weeks, she only had one shot to make this happen. She needed courage.

And she came through. The courage took over and in the last two weeks she ran a 15:57 and a 15:45, and fulfilled the last requirement to earn her black belt!

#4. Self Defense

When I was a young boy my DAD taught me to run away. It was a devastating mistake for a father to teach his son not to defend himself. I endured some very rough years

Chris Royce

from 7th to 10th grade. Being skinny, with red hair, braces and glasses made me a likely target, not to mention I was a year younger than my classmates. (That's like a whole life time in puberty years!) In the late seventies and early eighties I don't seem to remember any anti-bullying campaigns.

> "Keep neat and clean.
> Avoid bad habits.
> Be faithful.
> And never take #!%* from anyone.
> -Rose White 1873

In fact, it was survival of the fittest in its purest form, second only to the great wildebeest migration of the Serengeti. Eat or be eaten in 9th grade gym class. It was even magnified in my particular high school since it was such a small district. We had 84 kids in my entire graduating class. We had 7th through 12th grade in one school!

I entered the 7th grade with much fear and trembling. I had heard the horror stories about what they do to the new wave of underclassmen. I was 12 years old and completely hairless, scurrying around the hallways with grown men sporting full beards. They had cars, girlfriends, jobs, and probably their own homes. What chances for survival did I have?

A little self defense training would have gone a long way. I managed to survive junior high, but not without major damage to my self esteem and confidence.

Thank God things changed after 10th grade. The summer of 1985 was spent working at a Kiwanis Camp for New York City kids. 100 kids at a time would come to Upstate New

The Most Powerful Man In The World

York to spend a week in the woods. I was on kitchen duty and grounds maintenance for July and August. The first day I met a dude there, named Jeff, who was going to be the assistant cook for the summer. There were 7 or 8 of us workers that would be sharing a cabin, and as Jeff unpacked, I noticed his black belt. It was tattered and well used, and I got the feeling he was serious about martial arts. He was 3 years older than me, and much bigger and stronger, but he was also very quiet and peaceful by nature.

As we talked, I felt comfortable telling him about my challenges with being bullied over the past few years and he seemed to really care. He was sincerely angered by the fact that I felt I had to just take it, and I wasn't able to defend myself. That summer he agreed to become my teacher. The first thing that changed was what I would allow someone to say or do to me. Within a couple weeks I no longer believed I had to endure what other kids were dishing out. I could choose not to accept this behavior. Essentially, I just needed to be told I had that power.

Something my DAD never did.

Secondly, my ability changed. I was actually a pretty decent fighter. I was coordinated, fast, and I understood the moves and techniques. Knees and elbows work well for skinny kids, and once you know how to punch and kick, you realize power doesn't only come from big muscles. And thirdly, because of getting punched, kicked, thrown around and knocked out, my fear went away. By the end of the summer, I knew no one who was bullying me before was going to be doing it again.

I entered 11th grade with a whole new perspective. I certainly didn't want trouble, but I was ready to stand up for myself as soon as necessary. Surprisingly, the main culprits from 10th grade were friendly at the beginning of 11th grade. I guess they just grew up over the summer. However, a few months into the year, an older, bigger guy named Ricky decided to take one of my books in class, since he forgot his. His exact words were, "I'm using it, it's mine now." Classic.

I simply walked over to his desk and took it back, and said, "No, you're not."

He was rather shocked. When I sat down he let me, and everyone in the room, know that I was "dead" after class. On the way out, he came up behind me and dropped a shoulder into my back, knocking me into the lockers, and my books and everything on the floor. Three classes were letting out in the area, so we had an instant audience. I looked up at him and said, "I don't want any trouble, are you sure you want to do this?"

His answer was a jab with his open hand into my throat.

It's amazing what a few months of good training, lack of fear, and years of pent up frustration looks like when it is released. Poor Ricky. He caught hell. I must have hit him 8 times before his brain caught up with the fact that I was even fighting back. It turned into a good ole fashioned ass whoopin'. The teacher who broke it up and pulled me off ended up just as bloody as the bully. The string of obscenities I let loose is still floating in the hallway of Oriskany Central High School.

I am not an advocate of youth violence, brawling or MMA in the halls of our high schools. I am an advocate, however, of my children being able to defend themselves in a dangerous and violent world. I understand turn the other cheek. I also know this... eventually you run out of cheeks. We only have four.

I know my childhood life would have been exponentially better had my DAD instilled this into me at a young age. Then I never would have had to have been in that situation in the first place. The younger your children are when they stand up for themselves, the easier it is. The older they are, the more dangerous it is.

When my son Nate was 7, there was a kid who rode his bus home to hang out with another boy in the neighborhood. This boy, "Bo", was older than my son, and gave him a hard time. Nate was exasperated when he got off the bus. I told him we had a few choices on how we could handle it, and whichever he chose, I would support him.

#1: We could blow it off. Just forget about it.

#2: We could pray for him and let God deal with it.

#3: We could pay him a visit, and Nate could take care of business, and make it clear that he was not to be bullied.

He chose #3. So I said, "Let's go". He disappeared into his room for a minute or two and returned with some weird contraption, built out of legos, about the size of a grapefruit.

I asked, "What the hell is that?!"

His reply, "It's a weapon, in case I need it."

I said, "Put that stupid thing away and let's go."

Ultimately, when we went to the house where "Bo" was visiting, he wasn't there, and we never found him that day. But, as a DAD, I saw value in that process of offering options, letting my son choose not to be afraid, and me supporting his decision. Within a few days Nate came across Bo again. When he started running his mouth, Nate, in a moment of unprecedented verbal retaliation, threw out a mind blowing comeback.

It was, "Yeah, well you're a nipple."

This phrase was so senseless, so confusing, and so unique in the world of comebacks, it not only silenced his adversary, it momentarily silenced the entire bus. I guess there is just nothing else to say when you've been called a nipple. There's nowhere else to go.

#5. Kindness and
#6. Humility

Let me follow self defense with kindness. If you live your life with kindness you should rarely have to use self defense. Kindness is a defense in a way. Showing kindness as a man is not weakness. It's not being a pansy. I believe you can be kind and fierce at the same time. We need to be compassionate with our children, and walking in humility is a sign of true power.

That said, I have a friend who demonstrates great humility. He is a well accomplished man. He has a great family – a beautiful wife and three respectful children. He's successful in business; he's a retired NFL player who started for the Denver Broncos in the 1990 Super Bowl. Yet with all this on his resume', he carries himself with such humility. It's inspiring. When Warren Powers steps up to the podium to speak professionally, you feel the power. And at 6' 6", 265 lbs. there's plenty of power. If there is one example of humility I could point to it would be Warren Powers. Many men want everyone to revere them, but what they fail to realize is that humility will earn you more respect than intimidation, any day.

#7. A Competitive Spirit

"Our deepest fear is not that we are inadequate. Our deepest fear is that we are powerful beyond measure. It is our light not our darkness that most frightens us. Your playing small does not serve the world. There is nothing enlightened about shrinking so that other people won't feel insecure around you. We were all meant to shine as children do. It's not just in some of us, it is in everyone. And as we let our own light shine we unconsciously give other people permission to do the same. As we are liberated from our own fear, our presence automatically liberates others."

–From the movie Coach Carter

Wow! What a fantastic philosophy for life. For achievement. For fulfilling human potential. How does that make you feel when you read that? Read it again. It should make us want to rise up as men, and show the world what we can do!

On the contrary, how do these phrases make you feel?

"It's not whether you win or lose its how you play the game."
"Winning isn't everything."
"Don't worry about the score, as long as you have fun."

What a pile of crap. Last I knew, losing sucks. Winning is fun. The score matters immensely in life. Whoever came up with the concept of kids playing sports and not keeping score was not thinking of the future, or the reality of life on earth. Life begins as a competition. You began as the champion sperm. The one out of over 250,000,000 that got the job done! You won your very first race! I won the great egg swim of 1969.

Look around you. What about the animal kingdom, the forces of nature, the entire history of the planet? Good vs. Evil? Light competes with the darkness. The sun battles the clouds. Every creature must compete to live, and without pity or consolation. From the day they are born the competition for survival begins. Only 2% of sea turtles make it to adulthood. Only 3% of cheetah cubs survive. The competition in the animal kingdom is fierce and intense.

America has been a dominating world power for 200 years *because* we've kept score. We've kept score in athletics. In the history of the Summer and Winter Olympics the United States has earned an incredible 2,552 medals, far exceeding any other country by more than double. We have stepped up to the podium and received 1,018 gold, 824 silver, and 710 bronze medals!

We've kept score in business and commerce, in military might, and in innovation and medicine. Sadly, however, that seems to be changing. Keeping score and pushing for greatness doesn't have to mean cheating or taking advantage of someone. There is a mentality that has crept into our great country that suggests that winners are cheaters, and that everything should be fair and distributed equally. This is not how America became the greatest country in history.

I don't believe that being OK with losing gives permission for others to shine. It does not give our children an advantage in life to "not keep score." I do believe that we should be able to win and lose gracefully. Sometimes we do lose, and the appropriate response is "Good game". But we don't have to like it. And the appropriate response when we win is "Good game." I don't believe in breaking the rules, or winning at the cost of compromising our character in any way. I know that my quality of life is exponentially greater because my wife and I both have very competitive spirits, and we want far more than a participation medal for our family.

How do you foster a healthy competitive spirit without creating a crazy person in the process? Here are a few ideas:

1. Set high standards for yourself and your children when it comes to respecting others and playing fair.

2. Make cheating or poor sportsmanship a high crime, starting at a very young age.

3. Don't let your kids win too often. Make them earn it. No one lets you win in this world. All victories are earned in life. Of course this principle must be taught with a rational approach – I never let my kids win at board games or video games, and it didn't take long for them to beat me on their own!

When it came to sports or wrestling, I didn't beat them mercilessly to the point of total discouragement. Just use common sense... your 4 year old son needs to get the pin once in awhile! It's OK to tap out when your little guy gets a hold of your arm and twists it with all his might. That will build confidence and make him enjoy your "time in the ring" together!

4. Have family competitions and KEEP SCORE! Make sure you mix up the competitions so they favor all types of skills/strengths. Let each member choose, and run a mini Olympics, including mental and physical competitions.

5. Talk about how fun it is to win and share stories of your past victories, as well as other inspiring stories from history.

6. Never let your kids quit.

#8. Strong Work Ethic

I know men who will work from 5 a.m. until midnight to take care of their families. I know men who worked intensely for a period of time to build a business that now runs without them. I know men who have held down multiple jobs in order to provide for their families, and I know great men who serve our country in the military, and pay a huge price to do so. They all have honor. They all are good providers.

I also know men, whose company I do not keep, who are lazy and selfish. They are the men who do the minimum and who would rather watch TV and drink beer than improve their family's quality of life. They would rather take a hand out than work. These men are cowards. They have no honor.

I am so thankful that my DAD had a strong work ethic. He always had two jobs and served in the Navy reserves. (I do wish he had chosen a more profitable and enjoyable way to earn a living, because he never liked his profession.)

However, as far as work ethic was concerned, he was an outstanding example. He was not a lazy man. He instilled that in me as a kid. I had work to do, and it wasn't easy. I also had plenty of time to be a kid. I can't imagine it was intentional, but the balance was good. I appreciate the work he made me do between the ages of 7 and 15 or so.

By the time I took that summer job at Camp Kiwanis at age 15, my work ethic was solidified. The summers of 1984 and

The Most Powerful Man In The World

1985 permanently branded a strong work ethic into my being. Thank God.

"CIT" was an acronym for Counselor in Training. When Mr. Filliponi offered me this illustrious position one Sunday after church, I immediately accepted. I would get permission from my parents later! This was my chance. I would be staying away from home for the summer, sleeping in a cabin, making the big bucks, having my own money, and most of all I would be a part of the counselor in training program. I was in! I even managed to get my best friend Kevin hired with me.

What a summer we were going to have! On the first day we received our work assignments. I would be on kitchen duty for two weeks, and then I would move to grounds and maintenance for two weeks. I guess the counselor training would be worked in during the free times.

Here was my schedule:

6:00 a.m.	Get Up
6:10 to 8 a.m.	Breakfast Prep
8 to 9 a.m.	Serve Breakfast (100 campers)
9 to 10:30 a.m.	Breakfast clean up
10:30 to Noon	Lunch Prep
Noon to 1	Serve Lunch
1 to 2:30 p.m.	Lunch clean up
2:30 to 4 p.m.	FREE TIME
4 to 5:30 p.m.	Dinner Prep
5:30 to 6:30 p.m.	Serve Dinner
6:30 to 9:30 p.m.	Dinner clean up
9:30 to 12	Fool around, basic mischief, act 15

I realized rather quickly there were no counselor training sessions. It was more of an "observe from a distance and wish you were a counselor" program.

We kept this schedule Monday through Friday, and on Saturday we ended at Noon or so. I went home Saturday afternoon to do laundry and sleep, and I returned on Sunday evening to begin again. When we switched to maintenance crew, the hours were less, but the work was even nastier. We had to clean all the bathrooms. There were 100 filthy kids from NYC. Many times I wondered why we even had toilets, or why they weren't 5 times bigger so the pee had a better chance of actually going in the toilet. Either way, we mopped up a considerable amount of excrement during our tour of duty.

At no time whatsoever were we trained to be counselors. Now here's the best part... the money. After doing all this work, that rivaled any illegal child labor situation worldwide, we were paid exactly...

Wait for it...

$100.00

FOR THE SUMMER.
FOR THE ENTIRE SUMMER!

$50.00 for July, and $50.00 for August.

I worked for over 600 hours to buy a Sony Walkman. And I was pumped! So pumped, that I went back the next year and did it again. Only that year they took taxes out, so I received two checks for $47.53. (There was no cost of living raise.)

The Most Powerful Man In The World

I wouldn't trade those two summers, as tough as they were, for anything. They served me very well later on in life. My friend Kevin made different choices. He quit after the first week. Amazingly, more than 20 years later I happened to run into him in a grocery store. We were both in our mid thirties, and he was exchanging cans and buying food with food stamps. I couldn't help but think that he had probably developed a pattern of quitting, and had never solidified his work ethic as a young man. So my point is this: We have to model and teach work ethic to our children.

When Nate was 9, he said to me, "I want an IPod Touch." I said to him, "Well, you better get your buns outside and start touching some weeds." Pulling weeds is a great way to build work ethic and earn you some money for an IPod. I used it for my daughter when she was 8 or 9, and then she passed the mantle on to her younger brother.

I incorporated a few lessons that relate to work ethic into the exercise.

1. Quality matters
2. You must work under less than ideal conditions
3. Time management is critical

To teach these life lessons this is how I structured our arrangement. You have all week to get the weeds pulled from around the house. You can do it whenever you like, but when Sunday rolls around I am going to check the quality of the work. If it is done well, you get paid. If not, you don't get paid for that week. 80% won't cut it. There's no labor union to whine for you.

If you procrastinate, and the conditions are unfavorable by the time you get to the work, you'll just have to work in the rain, or the heat. If your friends want to play, and you've put off the work, they will have to come back later. This is how life works. Average quality gets you average pay. You have to get after it regardless of current conditions, and we must manage ourselves or someone else will manage us.

These are good lessons for our youth! Obviously there are more positive traits you could develop. These 8, however, will provide a solid foundation for a great future. They take a lifetime to perfect, so why not start as soon as possible?

The Most Powerful Man In The World

Chris Royce

anyone can be a DaD but onely one can be chris Royce.

Dad,

Dear DaD, I Love you so much and I will all ways Try to be There with you and I don't no how to discribe how much I respect you and Love you and long to go tears to a boot- camp with you.

Love,
Nate Royce

Chapter Seven

All Kids Are Broke

I am always amazed at how kids think they are rich. You hear them say, "I have a pool." "I have a home theater." "I have a whatever!"

No, **you** don't. Your **parents** do! **You** are completely broke, because **you** haven't earned anything yet. Your parents are just generous enough to allow you to use their stuff. You really only own what you earn in life. My daughter and son get to stay in their rooms that **I** own, for very cheap rent. (It's actually free for now.) They wear the clothes that **I** buy, and they eat the food that **I** pay for. They ride in **my** vehicles, they watch **my** TV, and they sit on **my** furniture.

They really don't own too much when you think about it. This chapter is about teaching our kids how to think about, understand, and handle money. Most of us were never taught these things, and the school of hard knocks for finance has an expensive and painful tuition. It can cost thousands of dollars to learn you don't get something for nothing. I took my nephew on a bass fishing trip to Mexico one year. He was 17, and it was his first trip out of the country. Halfway through our stay, I told him that one Peso was worth ten times our American dollar. The opposite, of course, is true.

He was convinced he could cash in all his dollars for Pesos before we headed home and make lots of money. His questions were easily answered and, with a gleam in his eye, he began to calculate his first profit in the world of international banking. His questions were, "Why doesn't everyone do it?" and "Where do I cash in?" My replies were, "Everyone doesn't know about it." and "You have to go to a major bank when you get home and make the exchange." I couldn't wait to see the look on the teller's face when he attempted to cash in a bag full of pesos for ten times the value!

He proceeded to convert all his US dollars for Pesos before we left. He was extremely excited to get his $800.00 windfall. As it turned out, there was a money exchange in the Houston airport, and the other guys and I watched with great anticipation as he went to cash in. The look on his face was priceless!

When we finished laughing and caught our breath, I asked the other guys a simple question that revealed my reason for the seemingly cruel joke. "How much did it cost you to learn that there is no such thing as easy money?" Both of their replies were the same: "Thousands." I then told my nephew he can thank me later for saving him thousands of dollars. He paid for this lesson with embarrassment and minor disappointment.

My parents worked hard. They were faithful to their jobs. My dad always had at least two. My mom had a Master's Degree. They left the house early. And they had no money. They earned it. They just didn't know how to keep it. They were classic middle class Americans.

They were never shown key financial principles that would have enabled them to build some wealth. They could have accumulated a decent amount of money if they had more knowledge and better habits. My wife's parents had very different views and feelings about money. They didn't feel it was important. They down played the need to earn a large income, and discouraged the ideas of business, profits, and wealth. These philosophies greatly handicapped my wife's opportunities growing up.

My wife and I decided early on that we wanted to create a life that was far from average and ordinary. The limitation that lack of income, lack of knowledge, and lack of resources created was far too frustrating. We decided that we did not want to raise our kids with the same limitations we had. Each generation is supposed to build on the previous, and get stronger, farther, and freer. Our parents got us to a certain point, and it's up to us to get us to the next level.

I am going to outline a few common misconceptions and truths about money. These are some of the financial philosophies that have served my family well. I will also explain some financial principles that most adults aren't aware of. My hope is that you will take a moment to equip your sons and daughters with basic knowledge of how to be responsible with their money.

Misconceptions	Truths
Money is the Root of All Evil	The Love of Money is the Root of Evil
Rich People Are Greedy	Anyone Can Be Greedy or Generous
Poverty Equals Godliness	Godliness Equals Godliness
Poverty is A Permanent Condition	Poverty is a State of Mind
The World Owes Me Something	Life is Based on Seed, Not Need *
Money Can't Buy Me Happiness	Poverty Can't Buy You Happiness Either
Hard Work Pays	Smart Work Pays
Good Education Results in a Good Job	Profits Are Better Than Wages
You Get Paid By the Hour	You Are Paid For the Value You Bring To the Hour
I Can't Afford To Give	You Can't Afford Not To Give

*You don't get a harvest because you're hungry; you get a harvest because you've planted one! **A harvest is better than a handout any day!**

Let me expand on a few of these misconceptions and truths. I know some very generous wealthy people. I know some very stingy wealthy people. I also know some very greedy poor people, and some very generous people who don't have much. So that dispels those myths! Make sure you don't make the mistake of programming your children that wealth is inherently evil, or that economic status is an indicator of the condition of someone's heart.

Fruitfulness in life is based on seed, not need. No one has a harvest simply because they are hungry. A harvest is a result of planting, tending, faith, and work. Good ideas pay good money. Value in the marketplace, solving problems, and effective marketing and distribution generate revenue and income. Mere want and need produce nothing.

Kids should be taught this at a young age. They are capable of understanding this principle. The earlier they are taught responsibility, not entitlement, the longer they have to apply it to their lives and reap the benefits. The "old school" way of thinking said that finances were private, and "to mind your own business." How unwise. Aren't we supposed to be developing and equipping our children so they can go farther than we did?

Business ownership is an incredible concept to teach children. Quality of life concepts like leverage, profits and passive income are critical. In my house we believe in ownership. Why work your entire life building someone else's dream, when you can build a family legacy of your own?

Let's say I work super hard at a particular company, and over the span of my 20 year career I manage to work my way up to CEO, with a half a million dollar salary. Not bad. However, when I am done, my son or daughter must start over. They cannot start where I left off. Hopefully, they create a great life for themselves, but there is no chance of them building upon my lifetime of effort, knowledge and wealth in that particular position.

If I had put that effort into a business that we owned, however, then at least they'd have the chance to continue from there. They may be able to take it from the half million to two million. The next generation can go even further. This is how generational wealth is built... if you're into that sort of thing.

If you take a 5lb. bar of steel, and turn it into horseshoes, it's worth $45. If you take a second 5lb. bar of steel, identical to the first, and turn it into needles, it's worth $300. But if you take a third 5lb. bar of steel, identical to the first two, and you turn it into watch springs, it's worth $3,000.

The same thing holds true with the value of an hour. Some people choose to turn an hour into $10. That's OK. Others, because of a learned skill, or trade, or an education, can turn that same hour into $50 or $60. Down the street, in a different neighborhood, with a longer driveway and a nicer lawn, lives somebody who figured out how to turn that very same hour into thousands of dollars...thru the leverage of business ownership. In America, the choice is yours.

I love what I heard the late Jim Rohn say at a seminar in California. "Kids should have two bikes...one to ride and one to rent." Entrepreneurship and small business are critical to the success of our great country. We should instill that in our kids! I also know that my kids may want to pursue another path. That choice is theirs. I just need to create the options, and provide a solid foundation of financial knowledge to help them pursue any career choice. I think we should give our kids ways to earn their own money, so they can own things!

> **"Kids should have two bikes...one to ride and one to rent."**
> -Jim Rohn

I don't necessarily think it should be from an allowance for doing things that they should do anyway. The way they get paid should mirror how they will get paid later in life. No one has ever paid me to keep my own house cleaned up. They should clean their room because it's the responsible thing to do. The garbage needs to be taken out regardless. That sends the wrong message. Pay them for what pays the most in life. We've paid our kids mainly for three things:

1. Overcoming fears.
2. Reading books. (Not fiction books!)
3. Teaching us something new.

These are the things that will pay in the marketplace. They are things that will lead to breakthroughs and prosperity. I also know the subconscious mind or human nature will try to solve problems in the quickest, easiest way, encountering the least resistance. (Remember my son and his request for the Ipod touch?) As I mentioned earlier, you don't get things just because you want them. It was a perfect opportunity to teach him a few great lessons. What we set up was a special deal to give him a chance to earn what he wanted.

1. He would keep the landscaping free of weeds, at the rate of $25 per week.

2. If the job wasn't done well upon Sunday inspection, he earned nothing that week and he still had to make sure there weren't any weeds.

3. He had to accumulate enough money to give away 10% (his choice where) and have a surplus after he bought the IPod touch.

Structuring his financial goals gave him a sense of pride and accomplishment, showed him that quality matters, and that he shouldn't spend all his money. I felt that this was a practical way to teach these lessons, even though I wouldn't normally pay him to do the weeds. He responded well. He got up early and hit the job each morning, many times before we were even up. He had a goal, a way to achieve it, and he was motivated. He earned over $300 before he chose to give away some money to help kids in the Dominican Republic. He saved some, and then bought his IPod touch. It was a successful process all the way around.

Another idea to help your children understand money and responsibility is to openly discuss and illustrate what you earn and illustrate what things cost. To do this you can use either real or monopoly money, and lay it out on the table. SHOW them what comes in, and what goes out. Ask your 9 year old how much she thinks it costs each month to buy food. See what comes back. This exercise will help you work as a team to manage money and resources well. They should know what it costs to run the house, and drive around, and be fully clothed!! They should understand taxes and insurance and investing. That means you probably should, too!

Here are a few key fundamentals that would be wise to know. After you learn them, teach them to your family.

1. How to build your financial house
2. The rule of 72
3. Be an owner, not a loaner (why tax refunds are poor stewardship)
4. The difference between whole life and term insurance
(see the resources page at the end of the book for suggested reading on this topic.)

Here are simple ways to understand and explain these principles.

Building a Solid Financial House

As we go through life, working hard to have money coming in and going out, our goal should be to build a well constructed financial house. Most of us are familiar with the building process to some degree. When we are building a structure, what is the most important part of that structure? The foundation. So we start with the foundation of our financial house, which is is called "Income Protection." Most people refer to this as life insurance, but you are protecting what assures you will have food, clothing and shelter- that's your income. Hence, " income protection." I have level term life insurance in place as this foundation.

Once we have the foundation in place, we have to continue to build the financial house in order. If you were to try to wire a house before you frame it, how far are you going to get?

Next in the building process is an emergency fund. This should be equal to three to six months of your income or your expenses. It's not a credit card. Using a credit card for an emergency is never preferred. It's not your money and it is too expensive to borrow that way. An emergency fund is just that, money you can access quickly for unexpected expenses.

The next level of your financial house is a written plan to control and eliminate debt. Debt is a big problem in our country today. What did the lending industry as a whole do for middle class America over the past several years when it comes to debt? Did they help people? No. We need to know some things about how to get out of debt quick.

> "Dollar for Dollar term life insurance gives you the most protection for your money. Period."
> -Kiplinger
> May 2, 2003

Debt stacking is a method of paying off your debts by making minimum payments on all but one debt, and accelerating that first debt with extra money. When the first debt is paid off, you immediately take the amount you were paying on that debt and apply it to the next debt on the list. You continue to do this until all debts are paid.

Then you have what is called "Savings and Investments." It is not short term, but rather mid and long term. This is retirement type savings. (Roth IRA, 401(k) plan, ect.) Then to finish the building of our financial house, we come to the roof- which is "Fun and Games."

Most Americans today are trying to build their financial house roof first, and they are wondering why it is in shambles!

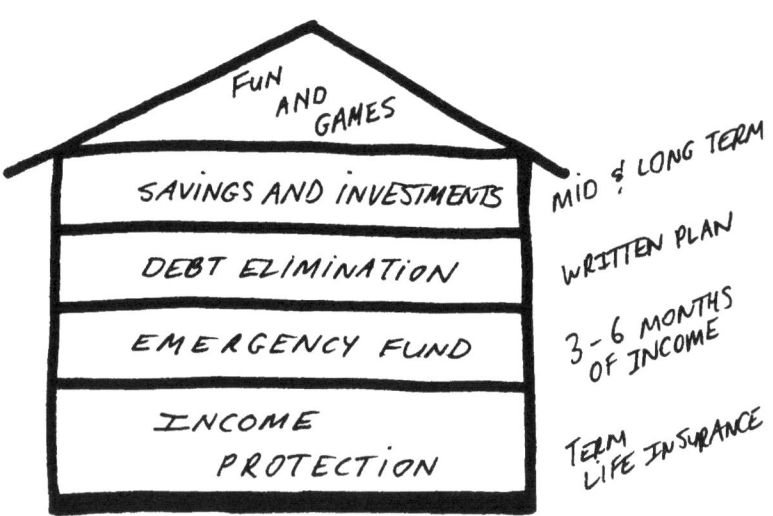

The Most Powerful Man In The World

The Rule Of 72

The Rule of 72 is an important financial principle that illustrates the power of compound interest. It doesn't show any particular investment, however it does show how money "behaves" when it is earning interest. In this explanation you will need three people to give money to as you draw it out, using their names, and three hypothetical rates of return for the example.

<u>The Rule of 72</u>

<u>3%</u>	<u>6%</u>	<u>12%</u>
$2000	$2000	$2000

I am going to give away some money today. Who wants two thousand dollars? Okay, Johnny, it's yours. When I give Johnny his money, here is what Johnny says, "Thank you for the two grand. I would like to play it safe. I am going to put it into a savings account at the bank because I don't want to take any risk." The bank is going to pay Johnny 3% in that account over time.

Who wants the next two grand? Jimmy. Jimmy says, "You know what, Johnny, You're crazy!"

"I think I can get 6% if I put it in a CD over time." I like to refer to a CD as a Certification of Depreciation. Here's why: The inflation rate averages 3 to 3.5%. The growth on a CD is taxable. So, if we are getting 6% and inflation is eating 3.5%, however the full 6% is taxable, how much money are we really making in the CD? Who do you think is making the money? The bank is. Well, Jimmy says, "You know what? I am going to put it in the CD," because that is what Jimmy knows to do.

Now who wants the last $2,000.00? Mary, you know what you are going to say: "Johnny, Jimmy, you're both crazy." I am going to put my money in mutual funds." What is a mutual fund?   A mutual fund is a pool of professionally managed money. So, instead of buying shares in only one company, which increases your risk factor, you buy shares in a fund. A professional money manager buys and sells the shares in the fund, which is commonly made up of 200 – 300 companies, so it spreads out the risk. That's what a mutual fund is. They were invented in 1924, so they have been around for a while.

To understand the Rule of 72, simply follow these steps. Take the interest rate that our money is earning and divide that number into the number 72, and the answer tells us how many years it takes money to double. So, if the potential exists to double money over time, shouldn't we know about it? Let's see how it really works. Let's assume that Johnny's money in his savings account at the bank is earning 3%. Divide that rate into the number 72 and the answer (24) tells us how many years it takes his money to Double. His money doubles and becomes how much? Two thousand becomes $4,000.00. Now if Johnny wanted his money to double again, how many total years would he have to wait? He would have to wait another 24 years, for a total of 48. How much money would he have? $8,000.00. That's it for his retirement. Sorry about that, Johnny.

The Most Powerful Man In The World
The Rule of 72

3%	6%	12%
$2000	$2000	$2000

24 $4000

48 $8000

Now, if we take the rate and double it from 3% to 6%, what happens to our bottom line amount? Will it double? Let's do the math. With a 6% rate of return, Jimmy's money doubles how often? Six into 72 is 12. So, in 12 years, he will have $4,000.00. How long before it doubles again? Another 12 years or 24 all together. Then he'll have 8K. How many years before it doubles again? In 36 years, he will have 16K, and, look at this, after 48 years, it's $32,000.00. Now, isn't that interesting? It did not double. It quadrupled. Everybody answers the same way. Conventional thinking tells us if we double the rate, we double the return. That thinking does not allow for the power of compounding. Einstein said it is the most powerful force in the universe, this power of compound interest. It's amazing.

So, that being said, let's take a look at Mary's money and how long it takes her money to double, assuming a 12% rate of return for this example. Twelve into 72 is what? Six. So, let's look at the doubling periods. She gets a few more. So, now I am going to test your doubling skills. (Then you run through the doubling 8 times.)

Chris Royce

The Rule of 72

3%		6%		12%	
	$2000		$2000		$2000
				6	$4000
		12	$4000	12	$8000
				18	$16,000
24	$4000	24	$8000	24	$32,000
				30	$64,000
		32	$16,000	36	$128,000
				42	$256,000
48	$8000	48	$32,000	48	$512,000

It totals over half a million dollars! Now, I've got a couple of very important questions for you. This is the same amount of money and the same amount of time, correct? Who is controlling Johnny's money? The bank. And what about Jimmy's money in the CD? Also the bank.

So here is the million dollar question. What was the bank doing with the money? The bank is investing into the economy. The bank doesn't keep your money in its vault, and they don't just use it for loans and loan it to your neighbors and friends for their cars. The bank invests and grows the money. They will gladly make $512,000.00 and give the average family back $8,000.00. The way I see it, that is a half a million dollar mistake. And when does your average family realize they made it? When it's too late. This is a concept your kids can understand, starting in 4th or 5th grade. They do math, they understand how to multiply numbers and they know that making more money is better than making less. Having a frank and open discussion with your kids about money, before they actually get into the job market, simply equips them. It empowers them so they know what to do once they have earnings. Don't you wish your parents had had that discussion with you?

Become An Owner Not a Loaner

Have you have ever received a tax refund? The average tax refund in this country usually averages just over $3000.00. So, here are a few questions for those of you that have received a refund.

Were you happy when you got it? (YES.)

Whose money did the government send to you in the mail? (YOUR OWN)

How much interest did you receive when he paid you back that loan that you gave him? (NONE)

How long do you guys expect to be in the lending business if you don't charge interest? (NOT LONG)

Why do people get tax refunds? Because they overpay. Does the IRS make us overpay, or do we voluntarily overpay? If we get a refund of $3000.00, how much did we overpay every month? $250.00. So do we voluntarily overpay Uncle Sam $250.00 a month because we just don't need the money? Have you ever had a month come and go where you could have figured out something to do with 250 bucks? Well, then, why do we do this?

Let me tell you the two reasons why people overpay. Fear and lack of knowledge. How far are we going to get if we make our financial decisions based on fear and lack of knowledge? See, we are afraid to owe. Nobody wants to owe the government, so we overpay, and we don't know how the things really work when we choose our withholdings. So, we figure we are safe just overpaying and getting a refund.

Now that you know the Rule of 72 and how to build a financial house, what could $250.00 a month do for the construction of that financial house? It could help with the foundation. It could help with the emergency fund, and it could help with the Roth IRA. That's money that we are just giving away to Uncle Sam and getting back, and paying debt we created all year because we didn't have enough money in the first place. That could make a big difference.

If you are getting a tax refund, my suggestion is to get with your tax person and make an adjustment, called a Circular E adjustment. Then work through your payroll office, and start getting that money to show up in your paycheck. You can then direct it towards building your financial house.

Spend some time discussing these principles with your kids. Implement them into your life, and begin to build a family legacy of financial knowledge and wealth.

The Most Powerful Man In The World

12/30/10

Dear Daddy,

    If someone asked me the question of... Who inspires you most?... I would say... My Dad. Not only are you a success in business and have the title of Worlds cutest baby, but you are more than that. A dad is huge part in a girls' life. Who else can encourage their daughter with the same power as a dad? Who else can give a girl the same feeling when they sit on their dad's lap? Who else can complete a little girls dreams? The answer to all of these questions is... No one except a dad.

    Not only have you answered all of my questions but you have managed to do it in a way that excedes my dreams.

    You will always be the one I go to for advice, and you will always be the one I go to when I'm feeling down. Your jokes and your smile put a spring in my step. You are dad that makes me laugh and you tell <u>the best</u> stories!

    You will always be known to me as, the best dad in the universe and nothing less.

Love,

Olivia

P.S. I cried through the whole time I was writing this letter because every word made me more and more thankful to have a dad like you.

Chris Royce

Dear Dad, ☺

You are an amazing dad. I love you very much and without you I wouldn't be the person I am today! (And I'm pretty awesome!) Once again you're amazing!

Love,
Olivia (Oli)

P.S. Thanks for the pretty flowers

Chapter Eight

Faith and Forgivness

I discussed the power of humility in an earlier chapter. Forgiveness is another very powerful aspect of world class parenting and being the DADS we need to be. Our kids need to know they are always forgiven when they screw up.

They are so eager to forgive us when we do. I am amazed at how forgiving little ones are towards parents that have been abusive or neglectful. It's after we grow up when we allow our hearts to harden against forgiveness and allow roots of bitterness to take hold.

My beliefs are centered around the idea that I have been forgiven by God because I have accepted the sacrifice of Christ on the cross. It is by faith in him that I am able to have victory here on earth and eternal life when I leave the planet. I also believe that there is power and authority in my right standing with God. This is not something that I have earned by being a "good guy", but it is something that

Chris Royce

I have accepted.

This life of faith is not easy, nor should it be. It is, however, exciting, challenging and rewarding. I am working hard to pass this on to my children. In a world of compromise, posing, and lack of peace, I don't know any other way to make it through.

Forgiveness is necessary. People hurt people. We will eventually say or do the wrong thing to our children. Be quick to ask for forgiveness, and be quick to forgive them. I realize that for some of you reading this book, it has been difficult at times because your DAD was not there for you. I know that many DADS fall short. I know that some of you were not treated with love and kindness. This was not your fault.

It is quite possible that your DAD did not get what he needed from his father. You are the one that can change the future generations for your family. In order to really do that at some point you'll need to forgive your DAD. In order for us to be forgiven, we need to forgive. The burden is too big to carry.

It takes real strength and a ton of courage to forgive the people who have wronged us, especially when we didn't deserve it. In the mid-nineties I had an amazing and life changing experience. I had the opportunity to travel to the former Soviet Union for two weeks. I did several very cool things while I was there, but I had one incredible experience I want to share with you.

I attended a series of week long evening meetings at the Stalin Theater. The theater was packed. Each evening there were speakers, performers, and music. It was all for one purpose - reconciliation. I watched members of the former

Nazi Party on stage asking for forgiveness and reconciling with concentration camp survivors. I witnessed the Jewish people forgiving them, and embracing them as new brothers in Christ.

Wow! Just remembering this day wells up a flood of emotions. So I can't help but ask... would it be possible for you to forgive your DAD? It will actually set you free. Yes, there is freedom in forgiveness, and to be great DADS, we need to be free.

One summer, I had an incredible opportunity. I had the chance for three generations of Royces to go fishing together. I bought a little fishing boat to celebrate the occasion. I flew my DAD in from North Carolina to Upstate New York. So Gramps, my 8 year old son Nate, and I headed out on a Sunday morning. The weather was perfect. For me it was like a dream come true.

After about ten minutes on the lake, my 70 year old DAD went to cast and he hooked himself right behind his ear. The hook went in past the barb, and was buried in the cartilage of his ear. When I got done laughing my ass off, I leaned over and helped him. I cut the line so it wasn't still attached to the pole. My son was completely traumatized. We calmed him down, then, accessing the damages, my DAD said, "You know what, let's not ruin the day. Let's just keep on fishing. We'll get it out when we get home." There was a little sinker hanging there, on 3 or 4 inches of the line, so I was calling him "Captain Jack Sparrow." He looked like something out of Pirates of the Caribbean.

He's a tough old guy, so we kept on fishing. As I turned my swivel seat around to start fishing again, I found one of the two big treble hooks on my lure was caught in the anchor rope at the front of the boat. (If you leave a lure unattended, it inevitably gets caught on something.) I wanted to get it out, but I didn't really want to cut the brand new anchor rope, and lose it. I grabbed a filet knife and started trying to dig that hook out of the rope. It was difficult because there was quite a bit of tension on the line.

As I pressed harder and harder, in my mind I knew I was doing something stupid, but I kept doing it. All of a sudden, the treble hook popped with tremendous force and went straight down the end of my finger, into the bone. It was so deep that the back side of the curve of the hook was over the end of my finger. I reacted like, "Oh my God. I'm hooked now!" I was trying to keep it from my son, but I knew I was in trouble. It was in very deep and I knew I needed to get to a hospital.

I've fished for a lot of years, and I've fished all over the world... Mexico, Brazil, Costa Rica, but I'd never been hooked.

I was trying to calm my mind and manage the situation so I tried humor, thinking to myself, my DAD and I are both going to the Emergency Room - hooked. I could see the ER team saying, "What the hell is going on here? You guys are morons." As I was managing the thoughts of thinking how I could get to the shore, I started feeling weird. About 10 seconds later I passed out- unconscious- taking a header right into the front of that boat.

When you pass out and wake up, you remember things in reverse order. I wondered why my feet were wet, why they were in the water. I muttered, "What happened?! Where am I?!" My DAD was splashing water on my face from the lake trying to wake me up. My son was freaking out.

The Most Powerful Man In The World

Then it came back to me. I remembered I was hooked, so I looked at my finger. The hook was gone! When I passed out and went over, the second set of treble hooks caught in my shorts and ripped the hook out.

So, the bad news is my finger was blown open. The good news is I was unconscious when it happened so I didn't feel it!

All of a sudden, I started feeling a warm, wet sensation on the side of my face. I realized I was bleeding profusely down the side of my face and neck. When I went over, I sliced my ear in half on the foot pedals of the trolling motor. My DAD said, "Son, you've got an ear flapper!" I guess that's a medical term of some sort, and he pressed it back and held it for a minute and it kind of stuck there. It took about 10 minutes to regroup, get my bearings and climb back up into the seat.

Then I simply said, "We're going home." It was ten after 9 in the morning. We got home, we got out of the truck and my wife, my DAD'S wife, and my daughter came out. "So, how was it?" We staggered out of that truck. I had a blown out finger, I had ripped shorts. I was covered in blood. My DAD still had a hook in his ear. My son had "dirt tracks" from the tears streaming down his cheeks. He just went directly into the house without uttering a word, and went straight to his room.

So that trip didn't go as well as planned. I knew I had a window of opportunity, though, to get my son back out there. We had to get back on the lake and get his negative memory replaced with a positive one. So I tried to refocus him on how God took care of me out there. I didn't fall overboard and drown. God came through. Sometimes things don't go as expected. Sometimes things don't turn out as we may have hoped, but there is always a positive side to focus on. You have a great future, and the past is behind you.

So my final thought, DAD, is this... Wherever you are in life, whatever you've been through, however good or strained the relationship with your children may be, however long it's been since you've seen them, decide right now today, for them, you are going to be the most powerful man in the world. Make whatever changes you may need to make, and jump in with both feet. They're waiting... and they are worth it!

The Most Powerful Man In The World
The Top Five Things To Pray About For Your Kids

Part of a DAD's job is to pray for his kids, and to talk to God about them. Here are the things I pray about for them the most.

1. THEIR DEVELOPMENT

When my wife was pregnant with our children I had a little pamphlet that outlined the stages of development in the womb and their time frames. It showed exactly what was developing each week. I used that to pray very specifically for the systems of their bodies as they developed.

I prayed that they would form perfectly as God intended and function at the highest levels. I included the nervous, skeletal, digestive, respiratory, and immune systems, as well as their senses. I asked that they would each be excellent in their abilities. I also thanked God in advance for intelligence, strength, coordination and dexterity, and I prayed for their personalities.

2. DIVINE HEALTH AND SAFETY

I am constantly praying for them to be healthy and protected. Everyday. I thank God for the angels that are assigned to them and go with them everywhere.

3. THE RIGHT PEOPLE IN THEIR LIVES

I thank God for keeping the wrong people out and bringing the right people into their lives. This includes adults and friends.

4. THEIR FUTURE SPOUSE

It's never too early to start asking God to begin to prepare the perfect match for them. I ask God that the path is cleared for their future family. The right spouse is critical for a happy life.

5. TO FIND THEIR CALLING AND WAY OF LIFE

I pray that as they get older their path becomes clear to them, and they find great joy and fulfillment in their work.

Start early and pray for your kids every day, DAD. They need every edge they can get, and we all need God's help!

The fruits of "getting back on the lake" and overcoming your fears.

The reason we've got each other is because we all love God. This family is perfect together. We make sure that we always are special to each other no matter what, by having family night and being together as much as we can. If we are ever sad or need help, we always, always help each other. We are the AWESOME ROYCE FAMILY and we will stay that way FOREVER!!!!!

Chris Royce

SOME ROYCE FAMILY FAVORITES

MOVIES:

Dad: Good Will Hunting
A Few Good Men
Gladiator
Dumb & Dumber
Pirates Of The Caribbean (all 4!)
300
Act Of Valor

Mom: Remember The Titans
The Notebook (of course!)
Forrest Gump
Sweet Home Alabama
Avatar

Olivia: Oceans 11
Forrest Gump
Stick It
Night at The Museum

Nate: I Robot
Transformers II
Avengers
Pirates Of The Caribbean
Star Wars

MUSIC:

Dad: Bob Marley
Christafari
Boogie Down Productions
RUN DMC
Eric B. & Rakim
Van Halen
Sade

Mom: John Mayer
Steve Miller Band
Sade
Boston
Van Halen

Olivia: Jason Mraz
Journey

Nate: Bob Marley
Christafari
Jason Mraz
Kanye West

The Most Powerful Man In The World

ROYCE FAMILY RANDOM LIST OF REALLY CRAPPY THINGS

1. Petting zoos (Why would I want to pet a nasty, wet sheep?)

2. Bus tours of any kind (Especially in other countries)

3. Fat hairy dudes in speedos at the beach (Or anywhere for that matter)

4. Elementary school concerts (Some kid in a turtleneck & sweater vest always barfs)

5. Long lines at amusement parks (A three hour wait for a three minute ride?)

6. Mini submarine rides (Claustrophobia and motion sickness all for one low price)

7. Hair in your food (I don't care how "clean" it is)

8. Claw grabber arcade games (There's nothing more exciting than a one in 10,000 chance to win a stuffed Sponge Bob Square Pants pillow)

9. Drunken sports fans in front of or behind you (If I wanted beer down my neck, I would pour it there myself)

10. Movie talkers (I paid to hear the actors, not you)

11. Loud candy wrappers (Who decided to sell movie candy in the noisiest possible packaging?)

12. Lipstick on teeth (Um...awkward)

13. B.O. on the elevator (I hate it when it gets in the back of your throat)

14. Fart tubes (Our name for airplanes, since that's exactly what they are, large metal tubes filled with hundreds of farts)

15. Squirrels (They are vile little creatures that steal and cheat their way through life)

Chris Royce

TO ORDER MORE COPIES OF
"THE MOST POWERFUL MAN IN THE WORLD"

www.YOU-DAD.com

SPREAD THE WORD AND ORDER A FEW COPIES
FOR THE DADS IN YOUR LIFE!

The Most Powerful Man In The World

Some other valuable resources for you, DAD.

Wild At Heart	www.ransomedheart.com
Band of Brothers Boot Camps	www.bootcampdetails.com
	www.bofbbootcamp.com
Cool Projects & Gadgets	www.jmcremps.com
	www.scientificsonline.com
	www.carolina.com
Another Great Resource	www.allprodad.com
Goal Setting & Achievement	Success Is Not An Accident By Tommy Newberry
Insurance & Finance	www.moneycentral.msn.com, August 2, 2000
	www.smartmoney.com Consumer Reports
	The ABC's of Making Money By Denis Cauvier and Alan Lysaght
A cool way to retouch and print family photos.	www.yousnappedit.com
Father/Daughter - Father/Son Adventures	www.JHRanch.com
Family Vision	www.family-id.com

by
Nate The Great